The Sacred Play
of Children

Edited by
Diane
Apostolos-
Cappadona

THE
SACRED
PLAY
OF
CHILDREN

The Seabury Press / New York

1983
The Seabury Press
815 Second Avenue
New York, N.Y. 10017

Library of Congress Cataloging in Publication Data

Main entry under title:

The Sacred play of children.

  Bibliography: p. 140
  1. Children's liturgies—Catholic Church—Addresses,
essays, lectures. 2. Children's liturgies—Addresses,
essays, lectures. 3. Catholic Church—Liturgy—
Addresses, essays, lectures. I. Apostolos-Cappadona,
Diane.
BX2045.C55S23 1983   264'.0088054   82-14867
ISBN 0-8164-2427-6 (pbk.)

Contents

62/31

Preface

To appreciate the liturgical and ecumenical context of the very thoughtful articles collected here, one must go back to the Second Vatican Council. During its first weeks in 1962 one most agreeable and providential surprise was the warmth with which the draft of the liturgical document was received by the Orthodox, Protestant, and Anglican observers. Even in its early drafts, the Constitution on the Liturgy proclaimed commonly held principles and doctrine about the worship of the Christian Church—and this it did even apart from its specifics of reform, which were intended directly for the Roman liturgy.

Happily the same was true of the completed Constitution published in 1963 and of the successive developments of the Roman revision of rites during the period after the Council. In all of these steps, participants from the other Christian communions shared generously. In particular, this was true of the first real revision of the Roman Missal in four hundred years (1570 to 1970) and of the Directory for Masses with Children (1973), which was itself a landmark for the Roman liturgy and which is reprinted in this volume.

Some of the thoughtful articles in this book speak directly to the providential unity of concerns shared by the several churches for eucharistic celebrations into which young children are genuinely integrated. All the articles reveal, moreover, how much we who celebrate the Christian liturgy with children can learn from one another in the different communions—as we have learned in other matters, from lectionary reform to the very art of ritual celebration. Our interdependence in liturgical renewal is now a commonplace.

The Directory for Masses with Children, based upon the new Roman Order of Mass, shares the limitations of other official documents: at best it can only open the doors, especially the door of creative flexibility in liturgical celebration. But it has also opened the way to profound reflection about liturgies with children, the kind of reflection that leads, like the articles gathered in this book, to authentic and living celebration. And, it must be said to critics on the far right, this development has led not to childish or even childlike liturgies but to celebrations that are truly expressive of faith and praise.

Underlying the Directory, again with direct relevance for the revised Roman liturgy but with wider implications, is the General Instruction of the Roman Missal. The Instruction is a lengthy document, far different in tone and purpose from the front matter of medieval and modern missals. It proposes to describe the eucharistic rite in great detail by an amalgam of doctrine, theory, norms, and pastoral directives. Understandably it is a careful and cautious document, but one characteristic has been too little noticed and is pertinent to both the positive potential and the problems of eucharistic liturgies with children. The revised Roman Order of Mass is a kind of nuclear rite, a base upon which to build. It was deliberately designed—and thus described in the General Instruction of the Roman Missal—as an Order open to diminution and enhancement, to simplification and solemnization, to ideal and less than ideal circumstances, to all kinds of legitimate accommodation to the characteristics of diverse assemblies of Christian believers.

This is the context in which to understand the Directory for Masses with Children, and indeed to understand what can and what cannot be done to accommodate the more usual forms and style of the eucharistic rite to celebrations with children. (There is an evident parallel in accommodating the rite for the Sunday Eucharist to domestic Eucharists and other small gatherings and to the exceptional cases of massive assemblies.) The Directory describes itself as a kind of supplement or appendix to the General Instruction of the Roman Missal. As such a supplement, the Directory opens up, widely and wisely, the terms of the Roman Order of Mass and the General Instruction so that the faith-filled potential described in the articles of this book may be sought. In addition, without trying to be a treatise on child psychology, the Directory formally recognizes the real issues that are raised for liturgical celebration by the participation of children. It also faces the challenge to integrate the children into the Eucharist of the total community.

As a slight historical note, it may be added that the Directory of Masses with Children perhaps reflects better the liturgical intent of the Second Vatican Council than does the fully developed Order of Mass itself. In other words, the quite basic rite and the invitation to creativity, adaptation, and paraphrase that are given in the Directory may, if thoughtfully implemented, better achieve the noble simplicity and the pastorally motivated clarity enjoined by the Constitution on the Liturgy.

The articles in this collection demonstrate that the Directory is only a starting point, as it was surely intended—for Roman Catholics, of course, but also as a strong and useful statement for other Christian communions. If counsel is needed as progress is made, it is a counsel to look back upon the Directory and reread it occasionally, along with the still pertinent General Instruction of the Roman Missal. Then the wealth of material in these articles will be all the more worthwhile and eucharistic celebrations with young believers the more authentic.

Frederick R. McManus
The Catholic University of America

Introduction
G. Thomas Ryan

In a world threatened by nuclear holocaust, in a culture often bordering on pagan materialism, in the midst of so much anxiety, Christians still gather to celebrate the Lord Jesus. Our sacred play uses music, poetry, food and water, scriptures, movement to proclaim a God whose life we share. This interplay of human anxiety and sacred play has existed in every century. In a sermon given 1500 years ago, Augustine said, "Let us sing alleluia here on earth, while we still live in anxiety, so that we may sing it one day in heaven in full security." After listing the pressures and sins of the world, he reiterates, "Even here amidst trials and temptations let us, let all, sing alleluia" (Sermo 256).

A prevailing attitude in every local church is that we are particularly oppressed right now. This attitude goes on to presume that once that man over there (sitting on that important pastoral post) and once that woman dominating the liturgy committee move on to another church, then community and a fruitful ministry can exist. Once the mediocre members are out of the way, then alleluia can be sung, then worship planning can move without obstruction. There was a parallel saying in Roman Catholic circles right after the Second Vatican Council: these changes will produce fewer members, but at least they'll be committed and thus of higher quality.

Any lowering of quantity has not given Catholic communities higher quality. There are just as many mediocre Catholics as ever, and the same is true in most Christian churches. We are always churches of the sinners. We cannot hold off our fruitful work and sacred play until the problems of life are fully resolved. Augustine said that in heaven we can finally sing alleluia in full security. Until then we play and pray and plan these celebrations as anxious, imperfect communities.

As pointed out in many of the essays in this book, the conditions for spiritual growth and for full incorporation in a faith community do not seem favorable for our children. We can no longer rely on "Christendom" to provide a faith/culture context. But, there are other more internal obstacles hindering the development of nourishing worship communities. Some Christians see no need for liturgy planning and consider time spent thus to be wasted or, worse, to be positively threatening. Perhaps they fear that the clergy will be ousted by an upstart laity. Or perhaps they expect their Sunday service to be an hour of private prayers, not a common rite of the living Church. Each church seems to have additional reasons to fear liturgical planning efforts. Within the Catholic arena, some say, "The Mass is the Mass is the Mass. Why fiddle with it? Why spend all that time, as if by human efforts we gain salvation?" But their time is well spent because, as sensate creatures, we need to create an environment where we can open ourselves to and respond to the gift of salvation.

The articles gathered here try to move beyond these anxieties and obstacles to the realistic preparation and celebration of worship with children. They go a long way toward positing these sacred rites in the correct context. They are not all "how to" essays, filled with recipes for the perfect celebration. Nor are they "canned" liturgies, ready to be opened and served on the sanctuary platter this Sunday. Yet they are eminently practical. They give perspectives useful in every setting, and they use graphic examples.

The essays in this book are both ecumenical and specific. Some authors consciously use general Christian vocabulary to describe liturgy with children. Others speak from their own worship context in terms that best express their particular tradition. Both approaches have value because it is good for us to visit another tradition, and listen to its vocabulary, its problems, and its potential. We can turn then to our own rites and find fresh ways of looking at them.

Half of the essays were given as papers at the International Conference on Liturgy with Young Christians. Sponsored by the Center for Pastoral Liturgy at The Catholic University of America, this conference surveyed and critiqued current children's liturgies. As these words were being refined for inclusion in this collection, experts from a variety of Christian traditions were invited to contribute their reflections. For the first time, Catholic, Episcopalian, Presbyterian, Lutheran, and Orthodox perspectives stand side by side to say that sacred play is important and that our children must be part of this prayer.

This book is carefully entitled The Sacred Play of Children. There was some apprehension that the public would misunderstand "play," or think this frivolous. We are about something very serious—the need for our young to engage in common prayer, to find their place in the Lord. This is just as important as it is for adults. It is sacred play, not just religious education. For years our churches have emphasized education, almost to the exclusion of rites and common prayer. But as Joseph Gelineau states, we exist as a people of praise and we play sacred rites so that our longing can be enhanced, so that our search for and in God can be fruitful. Again, Augustine can be quoted for a perennial truth:

> Why the Lord should ask us to pray, when he knows what we need before we ask him, may perplex us if we do not realize that our Lord and God does not want to know what we want (for he cannot fail to know it) but wants us rather to exercise our desire through our prayers, so that we may be able to receive what he is preparing to give us. His gift is very great indeed, but our capacity is too small and limited to receive it. That is why we are told: Enlarge your desires. . . . In this faith, hope, and love we pray always with unwearied desire. However, at set times and seasons we also pray to God in words, so that by these signs we may mark the progress we have made in our desire, and spur ourselves on to deepen it. (Letter to Proba, Ep. 130)

This is more than narrow education. This is the formation of open hearts. Thus sacred play educates at deep levels. It forms young and old as the People of God.

The authors have given of their time and reflections so that Christians who find community in so many diverse traditions can foster better worship amidst their youngest members. Thus may we all sing alleluia while we still live in anxiety.

Part One

CRITIQUE/THEORY

Is the Adult Church Ready for Liturgy with Young Christians?
Mary Collins

T wo primary school children were overheard in a classroom conversation discussing their religion lesson. The teacher's objective had been to broaden the children's awareness of the needs of others. As one of the resources for the lesson, she had used a Maryknoll mission magazine. In it were photos of African children with distended bellies, suffering from kwashiorkor, a disease caused by malnutrition. Later in the morning Freddy and Brenda had returned to the reading corner and were reflecting together on the pictures.

Freddy wondered: "But how can you tell if you're starving or pregnant?"

Brenda knew: "Easy. Look with an x-ray. If there's nothing there, you're starving."

Sounding the Good News for the Young in an Alien and Alienating Land

Humor, so we're told, rises from unexpected misplaced, misdirected, or inappropriate responses to situations. But the Freddy and Brenda exchange is not pure comedy. It reflects the high level of alienation within the lives of many middle-class children in the Western world at the end of the twentieth century. Hunger is a human reality most of them have never really experienced; starvation is incomprehensible. Yet these are the grandchildren and the great-grandchildren of immigrants who were regularly in touch with human hunger—their own—just two and three generations ago. Now children tend to be overfed. And they have been deprived of access to the memory of the hunger of their family as well as the human race. The story reflects another kind of alienation: the intrusion of technology into ordinary life, so that basic personal life processes are increasingly inaccessible to people. Reflection on liturgical celebration for young Christians cannot abstract from this cultural reality. Adults and young Christians alike are held captive by alienating structures in Western culture and by social institutions in the United States.

The fact is that the market in this land of plenty is full of things for producing liturgies for young Christians. Not all of it is really nourishing for Christian faith. It is not my purpose to provide a theological critique of such commercially available materials; nor to reflect on the current practice regarding children's liturgy; nor to focus on the *Directory for Masses with Children* which has occasioned our interest in the question of children's liturgy. My concern is to look at the interplay between liturgy and cultures. All liturgical events have a human cultural context which those concerned with children's liturgy must take into account. Both the social sciences and the traditional Christian faith can tell us something about the limits of our present understanding of liturgy for children.

The current dominant values of American society breed attitudes of hostility which result in the exploitation and rejection of children. Liturgical celebration and catechesis which avoid that cultural fact are bound to estrange the young from the Church. To register this charge is not to claim that social hostility toward the young is either new or indigenous to our culture. It is an unfortunate human reality. Our interest must be in recognizing its manifestations in our lives.

The exploitation of children is often for financial gain. Such exploitation is sometimes crass, sometimes subtle, but it is pervasive in the dominant culture. While adults still respond with outrage at the disclosure of the phenomena of pornography, prostitution, and family-promoted sexual abuse of children, too many have adjusted to the inevitable attacks on young people's physical and emotional health through commercially lucrative sales of sugar-saturated foods, alcoholic beverages, tobacco, and other drugs. Our rhetoric laments this as a permissive society which puts almost no restrictions on our children. It is possibly closer to the truth to call ours an oppressive society which puts almost no restrictions on the ways we burden the young. It is adults who deprive them of constructive choice and victimize their weakness and dependency for the sake of adult advantage. Sometimes parents function as protective shields; sometimes they are the witting or unwitting violators of their own young. Most often parents are victims of a culture of alienation which they unconsciously accept as inevitable.

The rejection of children in the United States finds expression in a full range of ways. Consider the obvious. It is common to find urban and suburban housing laws and rental policies which exclude couples with children and threaten eviction to those who presume to have a child after they have signed a lease. Voters regularly defeat school bond issues. Equally common is the rejection of the claims of children on parental time and attention. Rejection of such claims finds expression in the physical abuse of children, in their neglect, or in their economic indulgence. This society tends to look for resolutions of conflict through violence or through money. The results of such rejection are devastating for the young. The May 1979 *Harper's* published an essay on the accelerating rates of the suicide of children in this society.[1] Suicide, the author wrote, is the ultimate internalization of parental rejection. The child, always wanting to please parents and win their approval, takes to heart the message that one's very existence is offensive. So one accommodates to the parent's wish by self-destruction. At least, said the author, children who are physically mistreated tend to struggle for survival. Other reports indicate that an increasing number of mistreated children turn to violence. In some cases, this violence may be directed towards their peers and/or adults. In those situations where the child is both mistreated and ignored, the violence may be self-directed.

Legislators reject children when they refuse to develop legislation which will provide for adequate child care for working parents. Employers do the same. Instead, the dominant society has agreed to provide and even pay for abortion, a manifestation of the social acceptability of the rejection of the young.

The society shows its hostility for the young in another way, by denying the young identity and a sense of self-worth. Our young must contend with the phenomenon of prolonged adolescence, a most bizarre time of passage, ten to twelve to fifteen years. During this time of social marginality, they learn to be consumers, encouraged toward indulgence in spending for themselves and indulgence in precocious sexual behavior. Reports from social scientists say that more than 50 percent of our young people have had sexual intercourse before they are eighteen years of age. Reports from social scientists say twice as many adolescents died violently at the end of the decade of the seventies as in the recent past, and that the death rate for 18–25-year-olds has risen significantly.[2]

Running this social gauntlet is cruel and unusual punishment. Increasingly larger numbers of the young collapse under the strain, and become socially deviant. Twenty-year-old collegians voice self-estimates and fears unimaginable to many adults: "If we didn't belong to a strict religious sect, we'd be degenerates and acid heads." Unable to face the possibility of foundering on the rock Permissiveness in their journey toward personal identity, many adolescents have impaled themselves on Authoritarianism and are clinging for their lives. But they are no closer to coming to personal identity and sexual maturity on their comfortingly secure perches. Nevertheless, large numbers are not ready to come down and take on what this society calls the normal life of an adolescent. In their confusion, many see no adults they can rely upon.

Why do I paint such a bleak picture of the current cultural situation regarding children and youth? On the basis of the evidence in published resource books on Christian celebration for the young it seems that those who are presently exploring children's liturgies have a romantic view of childhood and youth. Such a view actually denies their experience and ours. It also denies the young access to the mystery of our faith, namely that life's terrors and dangers are real, but our God gives life even in the face of cruelty and death. The children of the Hebrews have regularly had cultivated the memory of suffering, hostility, and death.[3] Why not the children of the Church?

A single book of more than a dozen commonly used resources for children's liturgy had a scenario for celebration that acknowledged and interpreted in the light of faith the concreteness of young people's experience of terror and pain.[4] "Birmingham Sunday: A Liturgy of Innocents" allowed junior-high-aged children to celebrate the memory not of Martin Luther King, but of four junior-high-aged girls, Carole, Cynthia, Addie Mae, and Denise, and all the other children of the world who have been victims of adult cruelty but who have nevertheless affirmed the power of life. A Liturgy of the Word let a message of hope resound through the words of a fifteen-year-old: "I see the world gradually being turned into a wilderness, I hear the ever-approaching thunder, which will destroy us too, I can feel the sufferings of millions, yet if I look up into the heavens, I think that all will come right, that this cruelty, too, will end, and that peace and tranquility will return again."

Exploitation and rejection, suffering and death, failure to show a clear path to identity and self-worth are as much a part of the cultural experience of our children as belonging and sharing and nurturance and affirmation. The focus on the latter and the denial of the former must result in a distortion of the message of salvation. Nathan Mitchell puts it succinctly, ". . . the Christian liturgy has never hesitated to speak, *simultaneously*, a language of sin and a language of healing. . . . The simultaneous presence of both languages creates a tension that makes genuine festivity possible. For unless festivity can deal with the unavoidable ambiguity of real life—its scabs and its successes—it becomes escapist. By insisting that we acknowledge our pain—our failure and our finitude—the festivity of worship offers us the possibility of moving *beyond* it toward a vision of humanity healed and reconciled."[5]

One author wrote prophetically: "The continued use of irrelevant forms of worship for children and high school youth can only lead to confusion, boredom, and ultimate frustration, rather than to a vital faith, life, and prayer experience."[6] Confusing, boring, and frustrating are apt words to describe much of what is now in print, the products of our first decade of efforts to adapt liturgy to the faith life of the young. Perhaps what has been happening on location in communities around the country has been more profound, more tension-laden and integrating, than what is in print. If not, we must reach for that depth as our first goal in the decade ahead. Otherwise we will be in danger of missing the opportunity to engage young Christians in truly "messianic festivity" which "struggles to awaken life, to intensify consciousness in all directions." And, since pain is inescapably present to human consciousness and life, "messianic festivity" neither denies it nor conceals it.[7]

Adaptation to the needs of children and youth cannot mean adaptation to their neurotic needs for denial of sin and suffering, nor to ours. Cultural adaptation does mean asking and answering the question: Given this culture, how must we live and celebrate faith so that the young may hear the good news of the saving work of Jesus and want to participate in the work of reconciling this world to God?

Bringing Childish Fear and Fantasy to Paschal Faith

A church which intends to celebrate faith with its young must itself celebrate the paschal mystery in its fullness. The Church must celebrate this mystery in ways that fit the human development of the young. If the goal is kept in view to lead the young gradually into deeper understanding of the mystery of life and death within which they live, one can begin to find resources for the tension-laden "messianic festivity" which culminates in the eucharistic assembly of the people of God, the fullest liturgical celebration of the one mystery.

Not all children's liturgy is eucharistic; but it should all be implicitly paschal. This is as true for children's liturgies as it is for the assemblies of the whole people of God. I am not talking about the language "paschal mystery" but about the depth of vision. Whoever lacks such depth of vision ought not to presume to exercise liturgical ministry for anyone, for this mystery is the heart of Christian faith.[8] Anything less than a profound liturgical ministry for the young is a betrayal of trust, another form of exploitation of the young at their expense.

Several years ago Nathan Mitchell wrote about the phenomenon of contemplative imagination or fantasy in the life of the very young, which itself constitutes a form of ministry within the whole Church.[9] He noted that children aspire to construct a world where despite pain and danger things turn out right after all. This hope for a world more real than the world they live in creates in the human heart a readiness to hear the Good News. The child wants, says Mitchell, what adults want: a deathless world where stories are what Tolkien calls "eucatastrophes"—stories with happy endings. The gospel is . . . the ultimate "eucatastrophe," the final fulfillment of all human fantasies about a world where things turn out right.

So, says Mitchell, the presence of children in the Christian community confronts all of us with a choice. It forces us to decide whether the fantasy that is the gospel is true and worthy of a lifetime's dedication in love, or whether it is false, another in an infinite series of illusions about a world doomed to inglorious extinction at the hands of stupidly realistic men. If the child is right, then the world has a future and so do we. If the child is wrong, then we should "all folds our hands and wait for the end with stoic composure." The child, says Mitchell, comes to the gospel through his fantasy and that fantastic aspiration can be brought to celebration in messianic festivity.

Child psychologist Bruno Bettelheim has written about the value to the developing child of hearing again and again tales of young travelers through life: the Hansels and Gretels, the Dorothies, and the ducklings, who face the dangers of wicked stepmothers, evil kings in castles, sorcerers and witches who cast spells that block life, and dragons that threaten to destroy it. Such stories acknowledge evil and danger but show the child hope for safe passage through it.[10] Celebrations of this hope culminate for the Christian people in the eucharistic banquet. But the signs for celebration of hope are everywhere. And so are the stories of hopeful events worth celebrating. Eventually the growing child must come to appreciate the sacred significance of the biblical story and the sacred signs common to Christian celebration.[11]

To the degree that the children of the Church have withheld from them in catechesis, in celebration, and in life the corporate confrontation with evil and resistance to its power by the power of God in the body of Christ, they are poorly served in their life journey in this or any other culture. Strictly upbeat celebrations create illusions. Such liturgies which lack tension and ambiguity may simply be variants on the simplistic situation comedies of prime-time television. The mystery proclaimed in Jesus is that the forces of diminishment and destruction are real indeed, but the power and purpose of God will ultimately prevail.[12]

Christians hope, says Paul, for what they do not yet see clearly. Children's liturgies which celebrate wholeness and reconciliation as present realities without attending also to children's very real experience of threats to their well-being, threats which seem not to promise hope or resolution, are denials of the paschal mystery, not celebrations of it. Liturgical celebrations for very young Christians must be informed by a paschal vision which guides their fantastic aspirations for a deathless world toward the good news of Christ dead, buried, raised, and present among us for the world's salvation.

Coming to Maturity in the Body of Christ

In all cultures the young have to deal with the question of psycho-sexual-social identity and roles. We must remember that our version of early and prolonged adolescence is a cultural invention of a contemporary affluent Western society. A dozen years or more of social-psycho-sexual marginality is not one of the inevitably recurring structures of human existence. Much of the world neither knows nor has to deal with the luxury and the terror of requiring of its young this extraordinarily long passage to adulthood. Parents, pastors, and the adult community of the Church want the outcome of this passage to be commitment to the faith within the body of the Church. Yet there is an important issue at stake which the adult community has been skirting: the matter of personal-social-sexual identity within the body of Christ, which is the Church.

Recent anthropological and sociological research have developed some pertinent ideas about the power of ritual activity to engage or to alienate participants in a ritual assembly. The work of social scientists in the area of ritual studies suggests that every human ritual assembly of a group makes affirmative assertions about the humanity and identity of those who are gathered.[13] It also makes demands on the persons so identified. Rituals do this symbolically and obliquely, not through direct assertion. To the degree that what is affirmed ritually is able to engage the participants, they will also be open to what is required of them as members of the group. One could express the idea simply: the desirable dimension of life makes the obligatory dimension acceptable and possible. There is a correlative to this idea. If what is affirmed about the humanity and identity of those who are gathered is not engaging and desirable, the cumulative effect of the ritual action will be alienating.

The British sociologist Robert Bocock has recently studied the phenomenon of the growing alienation of many Anglicans from official church liturgy. He contends that many still look to liturgy for critical life moments: birth, marriage, death, and burial. But he notes that such participation often tends to compound confusion and not to help ordinary people to deal with the ambiguity and mystery of their human lives. On the basis of his study, Bocock suggests a hypothesis: What causes this withdrawal from the church's liturgy is the dynamic in Christian liturgical action which separates people from their own bodiliness, their own humanity, in a full range of overt or subtle ways[14] at the preconscious level. But it does occur, and it works its effect. Many nominal Christians have expressed their discomfort of a Christian church which continues to be alienated from human bodily existence. They react to this implicit denial of their full humanity by withdrawing from the assembly.[15]

The adult Catholic community—lay, religious, and ordained—lacks clarity of vision about the mystery of the human person, male and female.[16] Our assemblies reveal our corporate confusion about human sexuality and its place in the mystery of salvation. The good news of human identity and human sexuality as part of the creative and redemptive work of a loving God is not clearly proclaimed in our assemblies, because we scarcely believe it. We have a celibate male clerical liturgical assembly as we have a celibate male clerical church. The Church has allowed the story of maleness to be told as a story of unrestrained dominion over the earth, including human bodiliness, for so many generations that we have lost track of the original story of the image. That story speaks of God's image in humanity male and female.[17] We have forgotten that the *ecclesia* is called to witness to the first fruits of redemption, the reconciliation which overcomes the sin of the world. The vision of God's covenant within all of creation gradually has given way to or been usurped by the vision of patriarchy, and male and female reciprocity has disappeared from the word of God. Reconciliation has become an incomprehensible message, not a saving mystery within which the people of God live.

Our adolescents look to the adult Church to show them a full humanity which presents models of psycho-sexual-social integration for male and female persons. Is it not possible that our own confusion about the mystery of human sexuality is a greater obstacle to the faith of adolescence than the confusion we have about when to confirm? It is clearly easier and safer for us to debate the timing of confirmation than to struggle together as a Church to grow in understanding of male and female identity and responsible sexual behavior. Authentic rites of commitment to a community demand that those committing themselves recognize a place and roles for themselves that are both humanly intelligible and also manifestations of the paschal character of Christian life. To the degree that we don't always make sense even to ourselves as a ministering community of adults with mature or at least maturing sexual and social identities, our young may have no choice but to dismiss us as insignificant guides of their journeys.

In this culture, personal adult identity is too often reduced to a capacity for consumption and a capacity for sexual relationships. The young are encouraged to consume and to copulate before they have learned to interact with other persons in a full range of human relationships. But they are children in a church with a received tradition of anxiety about human sexuality. What have we to say to them? Can we tell them about a sexuality which is both creative and redemptive?

The early twentieth-century canonization of the adolescent Maria Goretti has long been recognized as an attempt to offer youth a model counter to developments in Italian society. The holy martyrs of Uganda were adolescents lauded for their deaths in resistance to homosexual abuse. But our young live in a world in which the culture of easy adolescent sexual activity devoid of commitment is perceived as normal—the real world. Does the adult Christian community offer with any clarity the possibility of mature human sexuality lived out in relationships that are rich with mystery, both painful and healing, both consuming and nurturing, both creative and sustaining? Are there really people who live for others and mysteriously become whole themselves?

Our imaginations and our energies are drained by preoccupation with the wrong human, liturgical, and theological questions when we aim catechesis and liturgical celebration for adolescence toward "confirmation" or reconciliation or vocation. Confirmation belongs to the initiatory cluster, and our adolescents have been Spirit-filled members of the faith community most often from their infancy. Reconciliation is a lifelong process, not an adolescent preserve. Vocation should follow after the achievement of a measure of personal identity with the mystery of Christ as the mystery of one's own existence.[18] What is the sacrament which discloses this mystery? It is the eucharist, but the eucharist celebrated in the fullness of the sign "body of Christ."

Our adolescents have been part of the ecclesial "body of Christ" from infancy. Only in adolescence does personal sacramentality emerge as young people gain an active capacity for sustained relationships with peers, adults, and children which are marked by reciprocity and responsibility, by creative and redemptive living. Messianic festivity for the adolescent requires sensitive and honest exploration of the mystery that "those who would gain their lives must lose them." Such celebrations must help them have an image of the body of Christ which is intelligible to them at a human level: an image of a people who find in the mystery of Christ the possibility of reconciling body and spirit, male and female, rich and poor, young and old, friends and strangers. A humanly intelligible manifestation of the body of Christ must rejoice in incarnation. That incarnation must be expressed in the domestic Church and the local Church or adolescents will leave the Good News of Jesus as they have abandoned the "eucatastrophes" of their childhood fantasy.

The matter of a special sacramental event for adolescence is falsely formed when it is cast as confirmation or nothing. Many rites of public blessing of persons have risen in response to the reality of the actual life of the Christian people. That can happen again if we judge to be true what youth ministers are telling the whole Church, that there is a pastoral need for the special blessing of adolescents at significant points on their ten- or twelve-year journey. We don't need a new sacrament nor the distortion of a liturgical action which has another meaning. We may well need public blessings of the young person within the eucharist community "at moments in her life critical for her salvation" to use a Rahnerian formulation.[19] What might those critical moments be? We need to celebrate with the young their increasing visibility as persons living out the mystery of Christ in their own lives. The appropriate setting for the celebration of the sacramentality of the ecclesial body of Christ is the eucharist.[20]

We might learn something about the ritual possibilities and the problems of such a public blessing of the young from Mexican American Catholics who have begun to revitalize a traditional celebration of the fifteenth birthday of a young woman of the community, the *Quinceañera*.[21] In its traditional form, the moment of blessing is also a public presentation of the girl as a Christian woman who will in due time approach Christian marriage. That content has particular historical significance which will not occupy us here. I make reference to *Quinceanera* because it presents the fact of a culturally responsive public blessing of the young within the eucharistic assembly. The adult Church in the persons of parents and baptismal sponsors joins with the young woman's peers, her childhood and adolescent companions, to present her for the blessing of the Church. She is singled out as a person in her own right, approaching her future in the community in the company of the many who have contributed to the fabric of her life to that moment.

We've blessed our fields, our church buildings, our church bells, and our fleets at various times and places. We did so because we believed that the stuff of mundane life—brick and mortar, clay and iron—could become by the invocation of the Spirit signs of God's saving presence in the world. Why not celebrate with hope our confidence that the young people among us are becoming salt, light, and leaven, the body of Christ, by the power of the Holy Spirit within them from their baptism?

Catechesis and liturgical celebration with adolescents must be geared towards exploring the mystery of the body of Christ in its present reality and its future possibility for their lives. Catechesis and minor celebrations prepare for public blessings by exploring the mystery of incarnation—the human person taken up into the saving work of God. Adolescent catechesis and celebration must never lose sight of the mystery of incarnation, teaching the young Christians, male and female, to be at home in and reverent with their bodies, learning the limits and possibilities of their persons.

Consulting the Tradition in the Search for Direction

Cyril of Jerusalem, one of the bishops of the early Church, spoke in an Easter homily of the hidden power of the great symbols of the Christian life and worship. He encouraged the newly baptized, "Let the oil itself become your teacher. You were anointed with chrism, and you have become Christs."[22] Saint Augustine of Hippo in North Africa had a similar vision of the power of the sacramental signs. In his sermon 272 we read:

> Would you understand the body of Christ? Hear the apostle saying to the faithful: "You are the body and the members of Christ." If, then, you are Christ's body and his members, it is your own mystery which is placed on the Lord's table; it is your own mystery which you receive. It is to what you are that you reply Amen, and by replying subscribe. For you are told: "The body of Christ," and you reply, "Amen." Be a member of the body of Christ, and let your "Amen" be true.[23]

Fifteen hundred years later, their words constitute good advice to the whole Church in the early stages of liturgical renewal following the reform of our liturgical books. Let the signs become your teachers. Become what you are. It is your own mystery which you contemplate.[24]

It is possible to propose a concrete direction for catechetical work which heeds the advice of these early bishops, the call of Nathan Mitchell for tension-laden and "messianic festivity," and the call of the Vatican Council for greater clarity in sacramental signs for the whole Church. This clear and simple direction comes from some research and theological reflection I have done over the past five years on the renewed rites. This proposed direction corresponds with the basic perspectives of the *Directory for Masses with Children*, namely that celebrations must be concrete in order to open children to the perception of the mystery of Christ.[25]

Not a few people have commented over the years that such a perspective is a need of adults. This convergence of adults' and children's needs for concreteness in liturgical action comes to the fore in the *Rite for Christian Initiation of Adults*. Just as the *Directory for Masses with Children* also speaks to adults' liturgical needs, so also the *RCIA* provides a firm vision for those working with children and adolescents.

The *RCIA* sets out programmatically the basic cluster of the dominant ritual signs which occur over and over again in all of Christian life and celebration.[26] The basic tension-laden liturgical signs for messianic festivity accessible to Christian young, adolescent, and adult are the same, few in number, and to the degree that we—adult teachers of the young—are present to their mystery, these signs will indeed teach a paschal "habit of being" in the world.

What are the dominant recurring liturgical signs of the Christian people? The RCIA presents them as: (1) assembling; (2) signing with the cross; (3) salting; (4) proclaiming a living word; (5) laying on hands; (6) anointing; (7) illuminating; (8) plunging into water; and (9) sharing bread and wine.

How are we and young Christians to become present to the mystery of these human signs that are at the heart of Christian worship? We must explore and celebrate them in depth, in all their richness and ambiguity, in their human cultural meanings, and in their place in the story of salvation. We must explore their imaginative and significant use by the Christian people at different times and places in response to the circumstances of their lives and the quality of their faith.

Consider only signing with the cross. The *RCIA* presents this ritual action as the framing action for initiation.[27] It is the first liturgical sign with which the Church meets the prospective Christian, infant or adult. It is also the penultimate sign of the process of initiation. In the joining of cross and chrism the Church welcomes into the fullness of the ecclesial body of Christ the one who lives by the sign of the cross and the empowerment of the Spirit. Only then do all participate together in the mystery of the eucharistic body of Christ.

The sign of the cross under which the Christian people live invites "messianic festivity." It is a sign of contradiction as well as a cosmic sign of wholeness which has been recognized and used as a sign of integration by peoples everywhere. The four ends of the earth are drawn together in this sign. Renaissance artists saw it as the organizing basis of the human body. It is, according to Jung, an archetypal human sign, present in life, art, and religious iconography as an expression of the aspirations of the human psyche.[28] But the cross is also an instrument of execution and a sign of destruction, degradation, and humiliation within human history. The Romans hung Jesus on a cross 2,000 years ago. Cambodians hung a twelve-year-old boy on a cross for pilfering food in the summer of 1979, and the news services made him a universal public spectacle, a sign of contradiction.

Early Christians recognized the mystery of Christ in this tension-laden sign and claimed it as a symbol revelatory of their faith. Christians have marked all manner of things with this sign. Just as people engrave serial numbers on property and brand the flesh of herds to prevent theft, just as humans have circumcised and tatooed and raised keloids on their own flesh to identify their allegiance and their belonging, so Christians have marked the sign ritually on their foreheads with oil and ashes and human touch. They have traced it on their bodies and have designed their buildings so that they could gather within the sign. All this has been done so that they could let their lives be transformed by the meaning of the cross. Artists in the Christian tradition have heightened the power of the sign by emphasizing now one, then the other of the polarities held in its balance, the fact of diminishment versus the desire for and praise of wholeness.

But the cross is accessible to young people only to the degree that memory and imagination are engaged in the creative exploration of the sign both as humanly intelligible and as a call to faith and hope. The experience of the Christian community with this sign and with each of the basic symbolic acts of the liturgical repertoire constitutes an abundant and almost inexhaustible resource for opening up the paschal vision and the paschal habit of being which is the core content of Christian life and liturgy.

The late Margaret Mead warned Catholics, in an address she gave at Catholic University in the 1960s, that the American culture lacked the capacity for ritual, because Americans did not value the stuff of which rites are made. One characteristic of good ritual is redundancy, the presentation of a single reality in multiple "languages" or expressive forms. Another is repetition, the valued and sanctioned recurrence of significant tension-laden behavior.[29] Mead was indeed prophetic in speaking a word of warning and judgment that needs resounding among us again.

Liturgists for the young, like all of us in a consumer culture, tend to look for and to want to create novelty, not depth of significance. Ritual redundancy and repetition are not of themselves inherently boring unless they are the activities of boring people who lack both memory and imagination. For those who are alive to life and those who are coming to life in Christ, the capacity of the human mind to act as a great transformer of the stuff of human life into signs of salvation should not be underestimated. But people need to be tutored in Christ in order to be set free.

The athlete and the dancer first discipline themselves in order to appropriate a tradition of movement, rhythm, and order. Only then are they free to improvise and go beyond the established forms. Adults who were not themselves disciplined by and who have not appropriated the great Christian ritual symbols and biblical stories that disclose the paschal mystery are not yet

free to improvise, to create and to innovate ritually to bring children to celebration.

Therefore, it was sobering to discover that none of the earliest books published on children's liturgies listed among their bibliographic resources either the *General Instruction on the Roman Missal* or any of the texts of the revised sacramental rites. Were these dismissed by catechists, rejected as irrelevant, or taken for granted? Internal evidence in books on children's liturgy suggests that their basic content has not been mastered. It is, for example, a truism among professional liturgiologists, at least ever since Gregory Dix, that the basic structure of eucharistic action is take/bless/break/eat and drink.[30] Yet only one of the dozen books consulted reflected awareness of that ritual structure of the Liturgy of the Eucharist and explored its meaning with young Christians.

Which brings us back to Freddy and Brenda. Look carefully: where there is no new life growing, the community may be bloated—but starving.

NOTES

1. Spencer Scott, "Childhood's End," *Harpers* 258 (May 1979): 16–19, The number of children who attempted suicide in 1978 has been placed at anywhere from a quarter of a million to half a million. (17)

2. "U.S. Reports in Death Rate Among Youth," *The Washington Post*, August 5, 1979, p. A 10.

3. The Passover Haggadah is one traditional liturgical action through which children are overtly introduced to the memory of suffering. So also, children's participation in Purim deliberately engages them in the conflict and hope endemic to membership in the covenant community that is Israel. See for example, A. Millgram, *Jewish Worship* (Philadelphia: Jewish Publication Society of America, 1971). Most recently worshippers have been struggling to incorporate the experience of Holocaust into the mystery of covenant life. See D. Roskies, *Nightwords* (Washington, D.C.: B'Nai B'rith Hillel. No date.).

4. Virginia Sloyan and Gabe Huck, *Children's Liturgies* (Washington, D.C.: The Liturgical Conference, 1970), p. 186.

5. Nathan Mitchell, "L'Zikkaron," *Liturgy* 24 (July–August 1979): 14.

6. Maria Rabelais, *Children Celebrate!* (New York: Paulist Press, 1975), pp. 5–6.

7. Mitchell, p. 14.

8. *Constitution on the Sacred Liturgy*, #5: "Christ achieved his task principally by the paschal mystery of his blessed passion, resurrection from the dead, and glorious ascension, whereby 'dying, he destroyed our death and, rising, he restored our life.' "W. Abbott, ed., *Documents of Vatican II* (New York: Association Press, 1966), p. 139ff.

9. Nathan Mitchell, "The Once and Future Child: Towards a Theology of Childhood," *The Living Light* (Fall 1975): 436–437.

10. Bruno Bettelheim, *The Uses of Enchantment: The Meaning and Importance of Fairy Tales* (New York: Random House, 1976).

11. For a brief introduction and further bibliography, see Jerome Berryman "A Gift of Healing Stories for a Child Who is Ill," *Liturgy* 24 (July–August 1979): 15–20, 38–42.

12. The theme of the victory of Christ over the forces of evil is deely rooted in the rites of Christian initiation from the earliest period. For a discussion of alternative themes, however, see Gabrielle Winkler, "The Original Meaning of the Prebaptismal Anointing and Its Implications," *Worship* 52 (January 1978): 24–45.

13. For an introduction to this approach to ritual analysis, see Victor W. Turner, "Forms of Symbolic Action: Introduction" in *Forms of Symbolic Action, 1969 Proceedings of the American Ethnological Society*, ed. Robert F. Spencer (Seattle: University of Washington, Press, 1969), pp. 8–10.
See also V. W. Turner, *Dramas, Fields, Metaphors* (Ithaca, N.Y.: Cornell University Press, 1974), pp. 55–57. Also Roger Grainger, *The Language of the Rite* (London: Darton, Longman and Todd, 1974).

14. Robert Bobock, *Ritual in Industrial Society* (London: George Allen and Unwin, Ltd., 1974), pp. 30–38; 147ff.

15. See Andrew Greeley, *The American Catholic* (New York: Basic Books, 1977), p. 136ff., for research data and interpretation which correlates with Bobock's thesis.

16. See Rosemary Haughton, "Neither Side Seems Aware," in the *National Catholic Reporter* 15 (August 24, 1979): 4, for a response to the controversy over the publication of the study commissioned by the Catholic Theological Society of America, Anthony Krosnick et. al., *Human Sexuality* (New York: Paulist Press, 1977), and the subsequent letter from the Vatican Congregation for the Doctrine of the Faith published in *Origins* 9 (August 30, 1979): 167–169. She writes ". . . the older ways of describing that landscape are no longer useful. To a young adult, to poor people, to non-Western people both languages (Aristotelean philosophy and secular humanism) are equally irrelevant because what is being described is not what they are seeing."

17. Rosemary Ruether gives an account of the fortunes of the "image" theme in patristic literature. See Ruether, ed., *Religion and Sexism* (New York: Simon and Schuster, 1975), pp. 151–169.

18. In his essay "The Future of the Christian Family," J. Dominian identifies qualities he considers basic to a Christian adulthood that is capable of relationships of intimacy. See *The Way* 14 (1974): 276–87.

19. Karl Rahner, *The Church and the Sacraments* (New York: Herder and Herder, 1963), p. 41 and passim.

20. One could argue whether there should be eucharistic celebrations presided over by the bishop as the focus of unity and authority in that local church in which the young people are gaining identity in their own right.

21. Angela Erevia, *Quinceañera* (San Antonio: Mexican American Cultural Center. No date.).

22. E. C. Whitaker, ed., *Documents of the Baptismal Liturgy* 2nd edition (London: SPCK, 1970), p. 29.

23. Augustine of Hippo, Sermon 272, in Migne, *Patralogia Latina* 38 (1861), Column 1247.

24. In his essay, "The Idea of Christian Initiation," P. M. Gy notes that the fundamental understanding of Christian liturgical action involves initiation "by the mysteries" themselves, not instruction about them. See *Studia Liturgica* 12 (1977): 174–175.

25. Sacred Congregation of Divine Worship, *Directory of the Mass with Children* (Washington, D.C.: United States Catholic Conference Publication Office, 1974), #9.

26. *The Rite of Christian Initiation of Adults* investigated using as a working hypothesis ideas set out in Clifford Geertz, "Religion As a Cultural System" in *The Interpretation of Culture* (New York: Basic Books, 1973), and in V. W. Turner, *The Forest of Symbols* (Ithaca, N.Y.: Cornell University Press, 1967).

27. Sacred Congregation for Divine Worship, *Christian Initiation of Adults, The Rites.* (New York: Pueblo, 1976), #83, #270.

28. Carl G. Jung, *Man and His Symbols* (New York: Dell, 1968), pp. 273–276.

29. For a published statement of similar themes, see "Celebration: A Human Need," in *The Cathechist* (March 1968): 7–9.

30. *The General Instruction on the Roman Missal* (#48) offers a modified version of the Dix thesis; see also Gregory Dix, *The Shape of the Liturgy* (London: Dacre Press, 1945), p. 48ff.

To Celebrate with Children: A Developmentalist Approach
Jean Marie Hiesberger

This essay is an analysis of the two purposes of children's liturgy: to enable children to celebrate their faith; and to initiate children into the celebration of the adult community. It may be that these two purposes are mutually exclusive since adult celebrations are highly verbal, abstract, and impersonal, whereas children celebrate best nonverbally, concretely, and personally.

Who Is the Child Who Celebrates?

Any reflection on the purpose of children's liturgy, namely to celebrate the faith of the child, centers on fundamental questions: Who is the child? In what does a child's faith consist? What is this faith we are celebrating? Simply, we must know and understand children. Since ignorance of children by liturgists hinders and may even destroy faith, we must utilize the tools and research of child development.

Developmentalists indicate that there are significant stages through which children pass as they develop in cognition, morality, faith development, psychosocial personality, and the ability to perceive another person's perspective, in other words, to form community. These stages are universal, sequential, invariant, and integrate the previous stage or stages.

It follows that children perceive, understand, behave, and celebrate differently at the various stages of their development. To realize the implications of this growth and development children's liturgists need to study the acknowledged authorities in child development (e.g., Piaget, Kohlberg, Erikson, Fowler, Selman) and to apply their developmental analyses to children's liturgies.

The ability to psychologically cope with environmental space varies greatly from a five-year-old to a twelve-year-old, so the liturgical use of space should attempt to accommodate this fact. Attention span changes from one age to another, so appropriate additions and deletions to the liturgy should be made accordingly. Motives for "moral action" cannot be Christian prior to a certain level of development which should be reflected in penitential rites and homilectic reflections. The ability to perceive and appreciate another person's perspective develops late in the child's life. Young children focus on action, sensory experience, and personal relationships in learning and expression. They are unable to distinguish between reality and fantasy. Young children do not have the intellectual skill of abstraction, and liturgical language not only requires abstraction but the application of abstract notions to actions.

Young children use their whole bodies in celebration with very few words. Often, words don't have the same meaning for children as for adults. For example, for a young child a "lie" has nothing to do with morality. It is simply a naughty word. The child interprets lying, which is a verbal utterance, as being in the same category as obscenities and other language the family finds objectionable.

Since a young child confuses fantasy and reality, and cannot relate to others meaningfully, there is no experience of the effect of lying. In point of fact, the child understands that a lie is something you should not do, but the rationale is not that the lie harms another person, or of the consequences to friends or family. The child's attitude is an indication of the appropriate state of mental development not a lack of moral training or religious development. Yet words such as "lying" are used with regularity as though children share an adult understanding.

Research indicates that certain critical changes occur in the middle years. Children change in their capacity to perceive and relate to other people, altering the development and specific function of peer groups. At this time there is significant growth in moral judgment and interpersonal codes. Such changes make for different needs and abilities in liturgical celebrations.

The effect of liturgy on "middle years" children is different as participation levels alter; the receptivity to certain aspects of the gospel message changes; and prayer styles become rigid. These children have a different faith to celebrate than they did previously. They need different styles of celebration.

Erik Erikson, who has documented the stages of psychosocial growth, realized that the person is in a continual search for identity and strives to bring meaning to life in the social situation. Erikson believed in the integrity and responsibility of individuals for their lives. One could not blame everything on the past and abdicate personal responsibility for one's life. Erikson believed that a person's interaction with culture, personal history, and society interacted to form an individual's identity. It is not enough for the liturgist and the celebrant to have only an acquaintance with this theory, they must be able to apply it.

Liturgy should be a confirmation of the child's goodness, as well as an occasion to speak in words and actions of the Lord. Liturgy affirms the community's positive stance towards this developing child. The sacraments when celebrated with knowledge and sensitivity can be channels for the healing and development of the child. Liturgy can help the child during Erikson's fourth stage: the inner conflict between a sense of industry and a sense of inferiority.

Other child development theories can have concrete applications to liturgy. Lawrence Kohlberg's stages of moral reasoning define the concepts of justice which may be operative in the preacher's constituency. For example, at "stage two," justice means that the people who are the most useful should get the best treatment; at "stage three," good people should receive the best treatment; whereas at "stage four," justice means "the law embodies justice for those who obey the law and who earn the right to justice."

So for ten-year-old Davey, right and wrong depend on the rules set down by other people, a typical "stage one" orientation. "Right" is obedience to authority and the avoidance of punishment. In the absence of authority, "right" is doing what you feel like doing. At "stage two," "right" is doing what you want, not as obedience but in order to attain reward. A child at this stage (note an interesting change) understands right as conformity to stereotypical images of appropriate behavior by one's peer group. Right is the avoidance of disapproval of others, especially one's peers. At "stage four," "right" is defined by the laws and standards of one's society. Right is the avoidance of society's censure and the subsequent guilt.

The future work for children's liturgists lies in the application of the work of child developmentalists such as Erikson and Kohlberg. This is the critical issue: that liturgy be planned for the child as the child actually is (thinks, feels, empathizes, and forms community). The alternative is to continue planning liturgy based on a philosophy of being rather than becoming.

In a constant state of becoming, children are in the process of moving from one stage of development to another. Consequently, a celebrant must know not only where the children are but where they are going. Knowledge of child development provides some insights. The work of developmentalists should lead to reflection on the questions we ask with regard to the entire spectrum of children's liturgy: from our expectation that children should participate in a community action to the limitations that children bring to liturgy, such as natural levels of interpretations. There should be reflection on how we allow children to use their bodies in prayer and celebration, and on their limited skills for abstraction and universality. We should examine penitential rites, selections from scripture, *how* we tell the story in the liturgy of the word, and the length of the liturgy.

Any acknowledgment that faith is possible for children entails the realization that children need to celebrate their faith. But it can't be our adult faith
that children celebrate. Children are capable of celebrating at their particular
stage of development. If children are to do more than just be physically
present, if we want them to have a positive attitude for liturgical celebration,
then we must take seriously where they are now. Our task is to nurture their
faith, not to create obstacles for its development. As the document *Music in
Catholic Worship* reminds us, "Faith grows when it is well expressed in good
celebrations. Good celebrations foster and nourish faith. Poor celebrations
weaken and destroy faith."

Children's liturgy should be as different from adult liturgy as children are
from adults. This requires an understanding of who children are. There needs
to be a definition of children's liturgy which takes the child as seriously as
it takes the liturgy. As they move from one stage of development to another,
children are as different from each other as they are from adults. To speak
of children's liturgy is to speak not of one but of several different categories.
We have children's liturgies and children's adaptations. It is as if the adaptors
did not know that there were pre-schoolers, primary children, intermediate
children, and junior high school children. These groups are as different from
each other as night from day.

There is an incredible amount of organized research available on the social,
intellectual, emotional, and spiritual qualities of children at various stages of
development. But this data is virtually ignored by those responsible for
children's liturgies. This research is essential to the development of liturgical
principles and celebrations of children's faith.

Children's Liturgy as Initiation

The second purpose of children's liturgy is the initiation of children into
the adult community celebration. However, one should keep in mind that the
celebration of faith and initiation is not the only purpose of liturgy. However,
these two purposes are fundamental and demand consideration and study.

Children's liturgy cannot be considered apart from the adult community's
celebration. Any community whose liturgies are genuine celebrations of its
faith provides the essential model children require. Many times children
boycott parish liturgy not for lack of faith, but out of good taste. A vibrant
community of adults will gradually welcome children effectively during the
course of their growing years.

The initiation of children into the adult community is the responsibility of
the parents and the community as community. The quality of the life of the
adult community determines the overall context for all parish liturgies and
provides the nourishing experiences needed for the faith development of the
parents and catechists. Significantly, it is here that parents experience the

sense of sharing ritual and celebration of faith, which are the sustenance they require to be spiritual providers for their children.

By and large, children will learn to ritualize and to celebrate their faith as they have learned to ritualize and celebrate their lives at home. They will be ritual makers in the religious sense to the extent that they have been sensitized to daily interactions and drunk deeply of the important experiences of human loving, joys, sorrows, and thanks. This process takes place slowly and imperceptibly through day-by-day exchanges.

Children whose parents can embrace them and say, "I'm sorry, I was wrong. Please forgive me," will have the necessary foundation for comprehending what it is to be penitent. Later, the child will be able to ask a sibling's forgiveness for breaking a favorite toy. These children will begin to comprehend what the family is doing when it joins hands and prays, "Forgive us as we forgive others." When grown, this small child will relate as a penitent to a community of brothers and sisters mutually forgiving and asking forgiveness of each other. This long and important journey requires parents who are spiritually sustained and educated to the sensitive task of developing ritual makers.

The great prayer of thanksgiving, the Eucharist, will not only be enriched, but will take on a depth of maturity if the family has rejoiced in each other's presence with hugs, songs, and dances; if thanks are given freely and received in words or gestures; if parent and child have shared meals with laughter; and if the young know the feeling that someone cares. Human experience precedes both understanding and ritualization. The family offers human experience and provides some explanation: these are the first tastes of ritualization as a community. This is the stuff of which liturgy is made.

The richness of the home experience is primary in the formation of faith. The fact that a parish's celebrations are weak and anemic may say more about the lack of family celebration than about weak parish leadership. Parents, who have the critical task of raising and developing the family, must bring to the parish a sense of community, sharing, ritual, and celebration of ordinary life. The parish can't create these things, it can only build upon them.

In many instances, what is needed is simple consciousness-raising. Parents don't need to do new activities with children; rather, they might be helped to comprehend what it is they are already doing. For the most part, neither religion nor religious educators have attended to parents. They've failed to provide parents with the help necessary to develop that special liturgical readiness the child requires. The ritual importance of daily events needs to be noted. There is no need to smother these events with religious language; they need to be appreciated for what they are.

In the process of the child's initiation, the family moves from a central to a secondary position. The community has a new responsibility as the peer group moves to a central position in the child's formation. The catechist and the priest must be ready to provide the milieu of liturgy, especially the liturgy of the word, before this necessary peer association can occur. Providing the appropriate liturgy requires a knowledge of where the children are in terms of linguistic, cognitive, moral, faith, social, and psychological development. One wonders how many liturgists have these skills or appreciate their significance.

A frequently heard comment is, "I don't need to study about child growth and development, I don't need to learn that. I can instinctively relate to kids." While this may be true for some, there are about as many as there are celebrators who can adequately intuit all there is in Rahner or Schillebeeckx. The analogy limps, but the point is well taken. Inculturation places on the community the additional responsibility of existing as a vibrant community celebrating meaningful liturgies. Many young people opt out of community liturgy because what they experience there is neither community nor liturgy.

This effort is imperative for the life of the Church. It requires skill and training. Continued effort will affect many generations. In some parishes, the process of inculturation and initiation is haphazard. In others, the task seems to be given to the least skilled person. Remember that the two purposes of liturgy are to celebrate the faith of the child as child and to initiate the child into the adult community.

Several areas need clarification. In doing children's liturgy are we trying to allow children to celebrate their own faith or are we trying to introduce children into the adult celebration. Obviously we must do both. It is important that we be clear about what we are doing as we do it. Trying to accomplish both ends in every celebration expects too much of liturgy, children, and leaders.

The liturgy should either be truly adapted to the children, as not done heretofore; or eucharistic liturgy for children should be delayed and introduced gradually and infrequently. Meanwhile, children should be provided with frequent, numerous, and brief celebrations which are truly child-oriented on the life themes from the liturgy, such as forgiveness, thanksgiving, and praise. Eucharistic celebrations for children should be approached with the utmost respect for and knowledge of children and liturgy.

Liturgists need to be provided with more human experiences and greater understanding of children through a study of the developmentalists and the implications of their research on liturgical life. Religious educators must develop a deeper understanding of liturgical theology and be challenged to new ways of ritualizing with developing children. Celebrants require better education; would that as much publicity and educational effort had been given to *The Directory of Masses for Children* as was given in this country to the reception of communion in the hand.

Catechists need the food of good and varied liturgical experiences for their own growth. Often at the local level they are not fed by good liturgies and do not possess good liturgical background. When they instinctively know that what's happening in the name of children's liturgies is detrimental, they opt for classroom celebrations. What happens is that liturgy becomes associated with school; liturgy becomes pedagogy. In other instances, catechists who are ill-equipped are left to their own devices liturgically so the result is poor liturgy with children.

Catechists continue to stock their libraries with liturgical fun and games books. They believe that when we blow up some balloons, bake our own bread, and stuff the offertory with gifts we are doing good liturgy. They lack the necessary liturgical skills and knowledge. In return, they receive little or no help given the complexity of their task and are forced to do liturgy by default.

On an academic level, there is a need for communication between liturgists and religious educators. Liturgists complain that religious educators do not understand the liturgy and should ask the liturgist for advice. The religious educators reply with equal humility that the liturgists have little worth hearing because they are so far removed from where the children are.

In this country when there are joint meetings between religious educators and liturgists, they are held for the purpose of one group lecturing the other. The battle on these occasions is won by the most articulate argument, not necessarily the most important one. And the silence which follows just augments the distance between the two groups.

Can we not see that we are both about the Father's business? That we should be urgently concerned to let the little children come to him? And that our culpable ignorance and our professional pride are obstacles to this? In the meantime, children's liturgies are going on, being led by curates and catechists who could use a little professional help from both liturgists and religious educators.

Serious reflection must be given to what is being done in children's liturgy and to what is being done to and for our children. When we can begin to help them grow in celebration of their faith, we will know that the true liturgical renewal has finally begun. The lives of our children and the life of their Church tomorrow will be the richer for our efforts.

Reflections: Children and Symbols and Five Years after the *Directory for Masses with Children*
Joseph Gelineau

Children and Symbols

Sign and Symbol

The role of a symbol is not to be explained but to be performed. The specifically symbolic dimension of our liturgical celebrations is generally suppressed because we lay claim to a verbal interpretation of its significance. This general propensity to explain symbolic actions arises in large measure from the fact that the evolution of Western sacramental theology from the Augustinian theory of signs has been too one-sided. Generally there is confusion between sign and symbol.

For humans, signs are first a source of knowledge. From a tangible fact (a written or spoken word, an object, a signal) we proceed to a reality of a different order, given certain conditions which have been analyzed by linguistics (a code, a referent, a contact, etc.).

A symbol is much more than the means to knowledge. It is a point of encounter and of recognition. It is an activity that creates meaning and a free existential statement of position. It is a compact and a commitment that no verbal explanation can ever fully express. When a piece of bread is placed in my hands with the words "The Body of Christ," it is up to me to know my thoughts, to know how my faith responds to this symbolic act. It is for me to conceive how I will react and how this will change my life.

The impact of a truly symbolic act cannot be preprogrammed. It must ever be discovered and created. That is where the richness of the symbol resides: it is at the foundation of our individual and social evolution.

By explaining a symbolic act, one attributes to it a specific meaning, thereby excluding all the other meanings, and in particular the one that I was going to discover to be the true meaning for me today. It focuses on a given object the searching of my longing, which cannot be restrained without being destroyed. It limits my spirit to one meaning among an infinity of other possible meanings.

The process of a sign is to lead to a specific meaning; for otherwise everything means anything and nothing has any meaning any more. But the power of a symbol is that it is inexhaustible: by structuring my evolution, it is eternally a creator of new meanings and of new actions.

Once explained, the symbol is reduced to the level of a sign. It is no longer a symbol symbolic of a creative act, but merely a symbolized symbol that is part of acquired knowledge. This is necessary and useful, but it is not sufficient. Humans cannot do without the knowledge through signs, nor without the relationships structured by symbols. The two processes interpenetrate. The rite and the sacrament are symbols as well as signs. But it is clearly a great pedagogical error to treat symbols as signs only: it cuts them off from the existential dynamic of longing and from the relationship with each other. Instead of giving them the chance to be creative acts, it reduces them to knowledge to be stored away in memory.

Myths and Rites

Humans cannot find meaning in the contingent and fortuitous events of existence; we cannot define our place among them and our identity unless we are able to relate them to fundamental and structuring "figures." Such is the role that myths and symbolic stories as well as rites and symbolic actions have always played in all cultures and all societies.

The structuralization of the Christian faith, in a child or in an adult, cannot be achieved without the intervention of symbolic stories and of symbolic gestures. The essential function of the Bible, as revealed and fundamental truth, is to provide us with a store of symbolic stories whose key is the central figure of the death and resurrection of the Lord. The essential function of the liturgy, from baptism to eucharist, is to have us enter into the alliance with God offered to humanity through his Son.

Before there is any explanation, one must tell the story and celebrate the rite. One must trust them both, without attempting to find in them in advance the personal evolution that each one will later undergo in their light. There are no Christian "subjects" until the Easter Story and the sacraments of the new life have "called" us into being, have structured, created, and launched us into the adventure of the ecclesiastical Christian faith.

But one cannot put trust in the story or the rite without running the risk of estrangement, of distance, of vacuum, and of remoteness where the change might occur. A parable is a fictitious story which first carries us away, beyond ourselves, if we are prepared to accept it. When the story stops, when the parable releases us, we see ourselves from outside and differently. A rite is an unnecessary action which directs our longing beyond all desirable necessary objects. When the liturgy ceases, a shift has taken place. Another being may be born in the space thus dug out and desired for one's self.

To be a teacher is to induce action, it is to give one's trust, it is to admit that a distinct being will grow ever more distinct. Symbolic stories and symbolic rites are the keys to the pedagogy of faith.

Personal Reflections

The written word endures, the world changes.

Reading again the Roman *Directory for Masses with Children*, published in 1973, I expected to feel some regret as I do sometimes for the post-conciliar *Ordo Missae*. If the latter were drafted today it would undoubtedly be different on various points.

But on the contrary, I have marveled once again at the fact that this insufficiently known and imperfectly utilized document not only had not aged but that it had often been ahead of normal practice in Masses in which children participate.

I note first of all the manner in which it presents each moment of the Mass. It sorts out what is essential and indicates how it can be emphasized: the announcement of the Word and the common prayer, the Lord's meal and the prayer of the Eucharist—announcing the eucharistic prayers for the assembly with the children, which have been published in 1974. It points out the components that are more flexible, such as the opening of the celebration or the preparation for communion, while orienting toward appropriate solutions. It inculcates a feeling for the celebration, for its dynamic, for its pastoral and mystical import—useful not only for masses with children but for all celebrations of the Eucharist. It constitutes one of the best practical commentaries on the *Ordo Missae* of Paul VI.

I should also point out its pastoral feeling, its attention to the various persons who compose the assembly and to the human milieu in which these persons live. Other persons will appreciate its pedagogical sense, its suggestions for an active participation, for a gradual initiation, and finally the importance given to the symbols and to the mystery. Everyone who is prepared to read and reflect upon these simple and clear directives can profit from them. It is not my intention to comment on them. After a decade, this directory maintains its value.

But during this time society has continued to evolve. The social context in which children live has changed. I propose to point out some of these changes. It should be noted, however, that I am not a specialist in religious pedagogy, that my thinking is conditioned by my personal experience, which has been in France not in the U.S., and finally that my observations may be confirmed or disproved by future developments.

Community of Symbols

We have not yet evaluated all the consequences of the change that is taking place in the relations between the Church and modern society. This change is bound to influence our children's access to Christian faith. Roughly, this change can be characterized as the transition from a Church of "Christendom" to a Church of the "diaspora."

In Christendom, the great "models" of social reproduction constituted by the family and the school served at the same time to form Christians. In present social life, these institutions no longer have the same efficacy. In those families where the parents are deeply Christian, the children are seen to pick the most diverse options in religious matters. The family is crossed by the currents that are carried by the mass media, among others. As for the parochial school, created to insure the harmonious development of human knowledge and Christian faith, it is now opening its doors to non-Christians and to nonbelievers. And regarding the baptized individuals whom the school instructs, it is often not known in what measure they live their faith.

Christian faith is ecclesiastical and communal by nature. One embraces the faith by joining the group of those who, moved by the Holy Spirit, recognize the resurrected Christ as their Lord and Savior. Thus, if the social institutions which in Christendom worked together to integrate the child into the Church have lost some of their efficiency, it is necessary that the ecclesiastical community as such help the child along the way to adult faith.

It is not enough that what the child may have perceived of the ecclesiastical community be reduced for her or him some day to a sociological belonging or to a set of received notions on God and Christ, or to a code of moral principles, or to an obligation to follow cultural practices. The child needs to be immersed in a cell of the ecclesiastical body where the belief in the risen Christ lives.

If children find some of that in their family, in their village, or in their part of town, all the better. But parents, educators, or school friends provide only partial images. The total image of the ecclesiastical *"Koinonia"* is provided only by the assembly of those who meet in the name of God to partake of the good tidings, their goods and services, prayer and eucharistic bread.

So the question is: What Christian assemblies and groups does the child encounter? What image do they convey to the child? In particular, in relation to the Ecclesia, which is the Sunday assembly: How are the children received when they go there? Where are they placed? How do they participate? What images, what feelings are imparted there to children?

The renewal of local Christian assemblies, as milieu for the announcement of the Word, of communal life and of celebrations, seems to me personally one of the keys to the future of the church in the world of tomorrow.

Initiation to Symbol Community

I mean by "Christian initiation" the total experience of becoming a Christian. In order to be fully integrated into the life of the Church and to become an adult in the faith, one normally requires a fairly long voyage. We also know that the catechistic course comprises several aspects: knowledge of the gospel (catechesis), putting the Word into practice (Christian ethic), entry into the mystery through the signs and sacraments (liturgy and celebrations).

At the various stages of its evolution, the Church has established various paths of Christian initiation. The one which still is the pattern today for the core of our pastoral work originated in the great pastoral effort of the Catholic reform after the Council of Trent. The post-Tridentine model for the initiation of children was elaborated in a context of Christendom. It rests on two foundations: the baptism of little children, as a practice that was not disputed, and the catechism which was developed at that time.

Infant baptism and catechism at school age are the two foundations that assume the existence of three supports in society: (1) The models of socio-religious continuity that are made up by the family, the school, the parish; (2) A religious faith generally shared by the members of society; (3) A dominant respect for knowledge. Today, these three components are in critical situations.

Before the age of Enlightenment, any individual was expected to share the religious faith of the prevalent social group. In a Catholic country, Christian faith was taken for granted. The institution of the catechism was aimed at arming this faith with enough knowledge to protect it against heresy and error. Today the situation is very different. With the rise of unbelief in society, one can no longer take religious faith for granted in children. Before starting instruction, one must frequently awaken religious feelings, open the door to the world of prayer and faith. Rites and concepts that are prematurely imposed on a child who has no religion or faith cannot insure a Christian development. Hence, the need for a prior awakening to human values and for the pre-eucharistic celebrations which are mentioned several times in the *Directory* (No. 9, 10, 13, 27).

Meanwhile, the position occupied by "knowledge" in social integration is undergoing changes. In the course of its history, humanity has insured the social integration of the members of a group by means of rites, of knowledge, and of apprenticeship. For thousands of years, the ritual model predominated. It is the rites of passage and the rites of initiation of primitive societies that the ethnologists analyze. Christian initiation during the Middle Ages borrowed from this model. Little by little, however, knowledge took precedence over rites. This is seen in Western society between the end of the Middle Ages and modern times where science provides the impetus for development.

For many persons, faith consists first of all in knowing and accepting a set of "truths and concepts." But we see today a certain decline in the prestige of scientific knowledge. In fact, it is apprenticeship and technology that are taking the lead. Hence, the reaction of some children to catechism: "God, what can you do with that?" reflects this mentality.

It follows that children no longer blindly trust the rites, including the rite of Baptism they received as babies; that children are no longer spontaneously eager to learn about God and religion; that they are more inclined toward the data provided by experience.

All of this motivates us to reflect on a model for Christian initiation possibly based on effective rites (Infant Baptism, Confirmation, First Communion, Sunday Mass) and a teaching of the religious truths included in a school curriculum.

One is thus directed toward the core of any initiation, which is the education of longing, within a cultural milieu. Nothing will happen if one does not start by awakening the longing for God, the feel for spiritual realities; if one does not provide stages, landings, challenges, which alone can cause the longing to grow; if all of that is not done within a group of believers (culture) which by its symbolic stories (Bible) and its symbolic gestures (rites) imposes a pattern on this longing and gives it meaning.

I feel I recognize here a whole series of intentions and studies for present-day catechesis. But progress is slow owing to the resistance on the part of prior institutions and the attitude of the parents. It is difficult to lift the barriers between birth and Baptism, between catechism and school, between adolescence and end of initiation. On the other hand, no one can foresee in the abstract a new path for Christian evolution. It will be a task for the entire believing Church: seeking firmly in the modern world what can best support access to a full and living faith within the Church.

4

A Look at Questions for the Future: The Eucharist
Elizabeth McMahon Jeep

My task is to explore the future of children's liturgy and to suggest questions as well as possible directions. However, one can only explore the future after assessing the past. The 1970s were a disaster as decades go—full of bitterness, frustration, and retreat on every front! During the 1960s, we went about with enormous enthusiasm scattering seeds, good seeds, into every crack and crevice and touching every aspect of Church life with hope and change. It was springtime and we were confident that every seed would germinate and every plant would bear fruit a hundredfold.

During the long, hot, dry summer of the 1970s, we have seen the seed which fell along the footpath gobbled up by the birds; that which fell on rocky ground became scorched and withered away; while that struggling to grow among the thistles was being choked off. We are weary of chasing away the scavenger birds, shading the scrawny seedlings, and doing fierce battle with the thistles—only to come out, scratched and bleeding, with precious little to show for our efforts!

What, then, shall we expect to see taking shape during the '80s—is *anything* left to grow? Or, to put it simply, what questions regarding the eucharistic life of children must be answered by us in order to preserve that very life? I submit five questions and suggest some of the implications and possible answers to those questions. I do this to help you ask *your* questions for the future—those that your experience suggests to you.

Is it Legitimate, or Appropriate to Celebrate a "Children's Eucharist" at All?

This question is not new; it has been around a long time. It raises an important concern by calling into question the legitimacy of the energies we have poured into the enterprise of liturgy for children. Yet this question has not received enough serious attention. Perhaps we catechists, in our hearts of hearts, suspect that the answer will be *no* on the theoretic level and *yes* on the practical level. The American mind rejects such ambiguity and confusion.

The question of legitimacy becomes more insistent as the Christian community realizes with more clarity the dynamism of the Eucharist as the center of the life of the Church. When we address *this* concern, we begin to understand the significance of the question regarding celebrations for a particular group within the community. *If* the children celebrate alone, are we not creating a mini-Church for them?

Some argue that children live in a child-world and therefore need child-liturgies that reflect their specialness. I think that is a bad path to take. There is only *one* real world, only one Church, one faith, one Lord, one bread to be broken for all. Children are real people living in the same world we inhabit. Both adult and child do have special needs, unique experiences, characteristic symbols and languages. The child is not just a miniature adult who lacks a certain degree of experience and intelligence. Children are as much a part of the local Church as are adults, or the handicapped, or the imprisoned, or the engaged couple—all of whom form small communities, and need opportunities to worship within the context of their shared experiences. There is evidence that teenagers have more significant contacts with and dependence upon peers than with either the family or the adult world. Certainly, these young men and women need some opportunities for celebration in a peer context. Children's liturgy provides the occasion for the prayer of *their* community to be offered in *their* words, the opportunity for the *one sign* to be celebrated through *their* symbols.

The norm of the Eucharist is the bishop surrounded by other presbyters, ministers, lay persons, and children, celebrating, on the Christian Sabbath, the memorial of Jesus dying and rising, present and powerful: that is the local Church. *All* subgroups—whether St. Cyprian's parish or the fourth grade CCD class—celebrate the eucharist in union with, in communion with, that local Church.

The caution that our first question imposes on us is that our children must celebrate as part of the whole. The prayers, the homily, the variations and themes must draw them into closer communion, not only with each other, but with the larger community—not isolate them from the whole of the faith community. Practically speaking, this means that we keep the broadest possible range of celebrations in mind: Masses for groups of children with several adult teachers or moderators; family Masses in church where special attention is paid to making the celebration intelligible to the children present; Masses planned by children to which they have invited parents or other adults; and family Masses in the home.

Let us return to the original question: Is it legitimate to celebrate a "children's Eucharist"? These words must not merely mean: Is it theologically justifiable?; they also must ask: Are children's liturgies worth all the time and energy? Put this way, the question can become a more important one: Are the children's Eucharists draining off the talent and energy that *could* be spent and *would* be spent on the adult liturgies in the parish? It has been my experience that in every parish there are more than enough people eager to become involved in liturgy planning for all possible liturgies—for subgroups or for the parish as a whole.

Where there *is* an active children's planning committee, but none for parish Masses, it is *never* because the only talented people in the parish happen to enjoy working with children. Rather, talented people have found that the ministry to children is the only area in which they can exert some independent thought and creativity. Parish committees often break up in frustration, or are disbanded, because (1) priests feel their prerogatives are being threatened or try to dominate all the meetings, or (2) different rules apply to adult celebrations—no visuals allowed, no extra-scriptural readings allowed, no processions or gestures or rubrical changes allowed, or (3) their work meets with strong resistance from parishioners who are offended by change and outraged by anything that smacks of a political statement.

On the other hand, I submit that independence and leadership have flourished on the children's liturgy committees due to benign neglect from the rectory and the general patronizing of children in our society. This is not to say that there are not hundreds of priests who are really and intelligently involved in the catechesis and worship for children. And I do not deny that in parish after parish there are profound, vibrant liturgies for everyone in the parish. However, our task is to look at the Church of the United States as a whole and to arm ourselves for the future with as realistic an evaluation as we can produce.

It is my opinion that in the majority of parishes nothing at all is happening on the adult level, but that there is a small group of liturgists working with children and experiencing some measure of success, flexibility, and growing sophistication. Yes, there is plenty of evidence of the garish, the superficial, the theologically and religiously inept in children's celebrations. But for the most part, children's liturgists have now had the freedom to work at it for years; they have had a chance to learn, to make mistakes, and to grow.

My first question could take another form with different implications. Isn't it counterproductive to give them eucharistic celebrations of their own? Won't it create unrealistic expectations of relevance and high entertainment level and appropriation of the liturgy to one's group and use? Will it not increase the tolerance of the next generation for heterodox liturgy? Won't "anything goes" become a liturgical principle?

The arguments for allowing children to worship in their own language and to celebrate religious reality in their own symbols have been well made in the *Directory for Masses with Children*. I will add that children who learn to express themselves in their own words tend to become adults capable of expressing themselves in their own words; children who learn to express themselves in the words of others tend to become adults who look to others for acceptable words and for an acceptable self to express.

While coming down emphatically on the side of eucharistic celebrations for children, I must acknowledge the strength of some of the arguments against them. For example, it *is* true that an occasional eucharistic celebration for children in addition to the standard sacramental initiations is considered in some parishes and parochial schools as perfectly complete and adequate attention to the worship needs of children. This minimal service releases the rectory from any further pastoral concern and involvement.

It *is* true that people tend to accept anything and everything as fitting in children's liturgy, and that children in some areas are being trained to *expect* gimmicks, superficiality, and platitudinous homilies. It *is* true that many creative people find a safe haven on the children's liturgy committee and never join battle to force some improvement in general parish worship. In these cases, perhaps, the answer to the question, "Is children's liturgy appropriate?" might be *no*!

In most cases children should be given the opportunity and encouragement to join with their community in offering eucharistic worship to God. They belong to a number of communities: family, clan, neighborhood, parish, school, class within school, scout group, sports team, diocese. Wherever one of these communities shares a common faith and can be called together in the name of Jesus they should break bread together with whatever adaptations are necessary to make its true meaning transparent and personal. All Christians have this right. Children should learn to know the Eucharist as a familiar and meaningful prayer; they should participate in the constitutive prayer of the Church so they will come to know themselves as persons with full membership within the Church. Children's involvement in the eucharistic celebration does not diminish but rather enhances the communion of all the members in the one body.

Will There Be a Piety in the 1980s and Will It Be Eucharistic?

Old-style devotions (except in the Chicano community) have apparently died out. In my opinion, despite efforts to revive them, they will never live again because the ethnic cultural roots which nourished them are now too weak. At present, there is an apparent thirst for something to fill this gap. One path seems to be a superficial seeking after fads—a little yoga here, some zen there, a smattering of prayer journals, and partly a life-giving determination to keep looking till the native and natural emerges. In the meantime, we can distinguish three convergent forces which may shape piety during the 1980s.

First, the role of the American Catholic family has been altered. More and more, families realize that they have been left to their own resources to develop prayer forms which are comfortable, and to devise a religious view which is meaningfully related to life. The family is becoming normative for the development of piety, most specifically, for the development of children's prayer lives and as the source of children's religious images. The general deemphasis on devotions experienced since the close of Vatican II is only partly responsible for this shift. This healthy centering on the family has been brought about by the changed role of religious sisters in the American Church.

In former generations, in a more immigrant Church, our piety derived from the teaching orders of nuns under whose influence a significant majority of Catholic children spent eight or twelve years. Through their teaching, we learned a particular devotion to the Sacred Heart or the Holy Cross or the Sorrowful Mother or the Miraculous Medal or Saint this or Saint that. While these devotions gave substance and color to our piety, it tended to emphasize monastic and individualistic values: poverty, chastity, obedience, the prayer of words, and privacy. These forms and values were in turn supported in the home by mother, who acted as the bridge to the parish, and who found support in female guilds and altar societies.

Today there are few religious sisters who buy into that brand of piety; fewer children in parochial schools are being taught by nuns, and there are fewer children enrolled in parochial schools. Where else can children learn to pray? From whom can they learn a religious interpretation of reality? The CCD experience is too infrequent and diffuse to have much impact in this area. We are forced back to relying on the formative, normative impact of the family. We have been paying lip-service to this truth during the 1970s, while at the same time we have been acting as though all of salvation depended on hiring a clever DRE or finding an assistant pastor who could play guitar.

Prayer in the family—or piety in the family—has three main characteristics at the present time: candidly, it is thin (tentative, faltering); its celebrations are centered on seasonal festivals and life-events; and it finds its underpinnings in the Sunday Eucharist. What I am saying is that it is weak at the moment, but *eucharistic*, centered in the feasts, seasons, and Sundays. What we do during the 1980s can support this movement or thwart it. If we value this strengthening of liturgical piety within family life, then we will literally rack our brains to find ways to nurture it. At the very least, we should begin thinking more decisively about occasional celebrations of the Eucharist in homes; about the family parish masses (and not just masses-for-children-only); about celebrating life events in such a way as to make them intelligible to children; and, of course, about ensuring that the regular parish liturgy is celebrated well.

Second, no one could look into the future and neglect to mention the charismatic movement. For liturgists and catechists, this significant movement has brought both good news and bad news. On the one hand, it promotes a scriptural, wholistic, and neighbor-directed piety. In its best incarnations it is a strengthening force within the eucharistic community. But, sadly, at times charismatic groups seem to exert a contrary influence: fundamentalistic, self-righteous, individualistic, encouraging a closed, cult-like narrowness. The movement can be preempted by either trend: we must await during the 1980s a more definitive unfolding of the meaning of the charismatic movement for the Church.

Third is the movement and impulse for intercommunion among the Christian traditions. This movement will find (and is already finding) its inspiration in scripture passages regarding the Eucharist, and, with or without official sanction, groups in increasing numbers are finding the path to a single altar table. Whatever our local situation, regarding public and official intercommunion, we must not forget to teach the children that, in fact, all of us who eat the one bread are indeed one body. Whatever pain it may otherwise have caused, the withering of private devotions *has* diminished barriers between us and the other Christian traditions.

By being alert to this advantage, we can extend it by taking care that the way we speak, teach, and celebrate always reflects the *essential* and not the peripheral, the structural and not the decorative elements of the Roman liturgy. One practical expression of this would be to become less preoccupied with the changing themes of the Church's liturgy and more intent on the permanent dynamic of the gathering to share the holy bread and wine. In our efforts toward a children's liturgy we too often tend to treat the liturgy of the word as a kid show, and the liturgy of the Eucharist as essentially boring, repetitious, and anticlimactic.

Should There Be a Minimum Age for Children to Receive the Sacrament?

This question may create more of a storm than did any discussion regarding the proper age of First Confession because some people want to answer from the viewpoint of theology and others see the question itself as a threat to a time-honored and comforting practice. Two important events have combined to draw our attention to this issue: First, the abandonment of the sacrament of Reconciliation as a prerequisite for the first reception of the Eucharist, which allowed us to separate the preparatory catecheses, simplify that for the eucharist, and recompute—downward—the age of discretion.

Second, the publication of the *Rite of Christian Initiation of Adults* which has reminded the Christian Community of the essential unity of the threefold initiation rite—Baptism, Confirmation, Eucharist—and which clearly questions the validity of our current practice of spreading them out over a period of twelve to fourteen years.

Without building the theological case step by step, consider that (1) adult initiation is the norm for bringing a person into full communion with the Church; (2) the initiation of infants has been part of Christian tradition since the early centuries, justified on the grounds of children's participation in and by the faith of the community; (3) any arguments in favor of infant Baptism must justify infant communion as well (children too young to eat bread were communicated from the cup until the twelfth century when the cup was withdrawn from the laity, and infant communion was abandoned at that time); and (4) any argument for postponing full participation in the Eucharist until the age of discretion (whatever "age of discretion" means), can apply with equal force to the postponing of Baptism. In other words, one is fully born in Christ and welcomed into his ecclesial body whether one is an adult or an infant. But once part of the ecclesial body of Christ, why deny any Christian the full participation in his sacramental body?[1]

Personally, I would like to see First Communion restored to its proper place immediately following Confirmation which would immediately follow Baptism. This triple celebration would be followed by a gradual revelation and education regarding the sacrament by parents without essential dependence on books, programs, unconsecrated hosts, and, in any event, without any white veils or other impediments. Furthermore, I would like to see *no* compromises in the form of solemn communion at age six.

With that admission of bias, I will now mention some of my own reflections on this subject!

First, the Eucharist is a sacrament of growth, repetition, and continuity. It is the sacrament of the ordinary and the familiar, not the once-and-for-all event such as birth or marriage. It is offered to our incompleteness and dependence, not our perfection or achievement. We must ask, just how incomplete is it to be too incomplete to participate? How dependent is it to be too dependent to need or benefit from the Holy Bread? In the Eucharist we see reflected the sign of the *manna* given day by day; there would be no stockpiling, no waiting for suitable disposition. Should we then, ask our children to wait to eat until they have achieved the capacity to be schooled?

Second, the Eucharist is sign and sacrament of the unity of the members. It is the sacrament of the Churchness of the Church; the Church is the hope of the child for faith. It was, after all, in the faith of that community that the child was baptized in the first place. And so, it is in union with the members of that faith community alone that the child comes to know the Lord Jesus.

Like the disciples on the road to Emmaus, and like all of us, children come to know him in the breaking of the bread.

Third, the Christian Eucharist is the celebrating of Jesus' command of the paschal mystery, the mystery of his death and resurrection and ascension and continuing presence in his Spirit. This is the Christian story, that the Church gathers to remember and renew and celebrate. The shape of that celebration is a meal in which bread and wine are blessed and shared as a sign that all present are called to participate in that salvation story and that all are one! Our children learn the story from their earliest days. They assemble in parent's lap or by parent's side for worship, and there they learn that there are two parts to the experience. One part is "Mass," to which everyone is obliged/invited; the other is communion, which is separable and optional. This initial catechesis and experience of dislocation is never overcome. For the young children, the eating of the bread is dislocated from its blessing and breaking, and the profound meaning of the sign of eating is disturbed.

The earliest pleasurable, most-consistent natural act of the child is eating. From earliest consciousness, the child realized that it is his or her right and obligation to eat, and to eat with the family. However, when children come to church, they find that the command of Jesus to eat his body and drink his blood has been interrupted for them: that they may not have the privilege until they achieve an arbitrary and intellectual goal. The very ordinariness of the bread-sign is jeopardized.

What are the forces against any change in First Communion? First of all, there is the conservative march which must be recognized as a force with enormous power at the present time. It has already begun to repossess the modest changes that were made during the last ten years. There is a return of the bridal dress and veil, the money gifts, the single parish-wide celebration, and the restoration of question-answer lessons in preparation for the sacrament. These are only the superficial manifestation of that force. It springs, I contend, from many complex anxieties within the Church.

Old-fashioned First Communion is an object of nostalgia because it is a sign of ethnic celebrations. Without these ethnic Catholic rituals and culture, the Church seems, to those of us with strong ethnic associations, amorphous, neuter, vague, colorless, and above all, powerless. Old-fashioned First Communion is a sign of a better, more stable, safer time when men were men and women knew their place, when the United States ruled the world and Catholicism was the one true Church. It was a sign of the time when right and wrong were clear enough for a six-year old to understand. It was a sign of a less complicated theology when Jesus was simply divine, when he was simply and literally present in the bread, and when he could and did demand uncomplicated obedience and piety. That kind of obedience and piety was not only *possible* for a six-year-old, but was *epitomized* by the devotion of the six-year-old.

In retrospect, the old-fashioned First Communion ceremony can be seen to serve as a rite of passage: celebration of the end of innocence. Adults realize that after six the child's simplicity rapidly decreases, triggered by school experiences as well as natural growth and change. The family is still the center and support of the child's life and belief system, but friends become important. To maintain ties with friends and school and neighborhood groups, the child begins to diverge from the transparency of young childhood. This *must* happen. We would not want them to remain artless six-year-olds forever; yet we look for ways to capture and preserve and celebrate the age which is coming to an end. So we dress them in white clothes and veils, give them flowers, let them smile at the camera and their grandparents, and feel special, wonderful, and beloved by God and everyone else. After this day, imperceptably, yet none the less definitively, they move from the realm of innocence and irresponsibility to the domain of sin and law.

And what more logical preparation for this passage than a series of catechism lessons where the children memorize in their simplest and clearest form the laws of God in capital letters. In this context, the sacrament of Confession becomes attractive to the parent as a mechanism for continuing some control in the child's life; it is a form suited to the sinful, boys-will-be-boys life they are passing into. In this context the sacrament is well depicted as "Confession" rather than as "Reconciliation," because they have not become alienated from the Church. It has more to do with obedience to rules than membership in the eucharistic community.

I am not trying to caricature and exaggerate. I am simply attempting to describe the natural human situation which gives rise to a desire within the Catholic community to maintain First Confession/First Communion as it was known in this country from about 1920 to 1960. Yielding up these two sacraments to serve this need, however, must come at the expense of theological distortion, and liturgical loss for the entire community.

It is not parents alone who long for the good old days. Pastors of a certain stripe see the sacramental initiations as necessary occasions for reining in another hard-to-control group: parents who tend to get lax in their churchly duties. The mechanism is clear: if the kids aren't enrolled in the CCD program, they can't make their First Communion, etc. The more enlightened among the priests and religious educators express the same sentiment, in different words: it is good that parents should share the gospel with their children; they should do this all the time, but we can't expect that! So we must call them to the parish hall for three meetings to tell them what the gospel says, and to give them a book so they will know what to say to their children, and then assign a date for a parish ceremony so they have a deadline.

And what of the argument that it is so wonderful for the children to be important and special some times? Yes, it *is* wonderful, but why set them up to think of that one day as the holiest or most pious of their young lives? They are bound to fall from grace if that kind of "high" is identified for them as grace. Particularly since, as they will recognize later, the high did not have the ring of truth to it in the first place. There are more appropriate ways for the Church to give special signs of affection to the youngest members of the community.

Is the Church Willing to Take Children Seriously?

We Catholics put lots of money into our children, not, I fear, because we understand or value them, but consciously, to ward off their defection as young adults, and to keep the current adults, their parents, engaged in the parish. We give young people no role in the life of the community (except as acolytes) until they are married.

We will know that the Church is beginning to take children seriously in the area of children's liturgies when we are willing to seriously address the study of nonverbal expression; when we ask psychologists, linguists, educators, media persons, and persons who work with the verbally handicapped for help in learning forms of celebration which do not rely so heavily on the spoken word.

We will know that the Church is beginning to take children seriously when we are willing to give children a place on the committees which plan their celebrations. Not as token members, but as persons with some genuine responsibility and control over the outcome. Will they make inappropriate decisions, moderator or no moderator? Certainly! Anyone who works with children knows that whatever involves them has to allow for and even provide for a certain degree of wrongness; the inappropriate hymn, the inartistic banner, the awkward dance, or imperfect diction. There is no excuse when these flaws come from the inadequacy and lack of preparation of adult moderators; but when the particular hymn or reading seems just right to the children—then the adult must yield. They can be helped to celebrate well and authentically without the imposition of an adult plan or an adult standard of performance. If we do not start immediately to engage children in the development of their own liturgies, we will raise yet another generation of passive, frustrated, liturgical illiterates.

We will know the Church is beginning to take children seriously when we are willing to draw themes and homilies from the real facts of child-life. Children, like adults, need for the Church as the caring community to validate, accept, and confirm their experience.

We will know the Church is beginning to take children seriously when we are willing to demand, on children's behalf, quality and significance from the liturgy and its ministers. Then we will object when someone says, "It's only for the kids," or "They won't know the difference." We will draw the line and say, no more sloppy, ill-planned, unrehearsed songs or spur-of-the-minute homilies; and no more recipe liturgies taken from books and magazines.

What Influence Will the Developing Theology of Ministry Have on Children's Liturgy?

Taking children seriously goes hand-in-hand with taking ourselves seriously. Perhaps those who are working with children will discover that the ministry of the catechist is a legitimate and vital one in the community. it is a ministry as real and particular as that of presbyter, and certainly more solidly founded in scripture than that of monsignor or cardinal! Those who answer this call accept the responsibility for mediating the Church to those who have not been fully converted or fully initiated. They draw young people into communion with the living body of Christ. They are a sign and reminder to other adult Christians that they are the revelation of God's life to all who approach.

What does this mean? It means courage: the courage to work for the quality of the eucharistic celebrations of the children; the courage to learn to lead, to stand on one's two feet and object to the pocket veto from the rectory or the scheduling change from the principal's office; the courage to demand a budget; and the courage to challenge the macho attitude within the Church that catechetics and children's liturgy can be discounted because they are the realm of women and children.

It also means study. It means facing the inadequacy of our own education and taste, and our obligation to subscribe to the best material coming out on liturgy, on children, on theology and history. It means our obligation to attend workshops and seminars, and our obligation to demand more than how-to-do-it workshops from diocesan personnel.

And above all, it means consistency. It means doing *all* those things correctly such as finding the time to involve parents and children in planning sessions, staying after school to work with the student lectors, and organizing a committee to find or learn to bake appropriate altar breads. It means doing all those things because *they matter*. Consistency, for the children's celebrant or homilist, means attendance at planning meetings, time spent with children, and acceptance of frank evaluation of presidential style of homily. It means learning names of parents, teachers, and children, while refraining from patting children on the head or calling them cute or playing favorites.

And finally, it means that we start recognizing the primary responsibility and privilege of parents. They are not our helpers. we are theirs! They are the true liturgists and catechists; the dining table, not the classroom, is the sign and setting for a child's catechesis on eucharistic prayer. Parents are not, for the most part, ignorant, conservative louts who need to be bludgeoned and threatened into teaching lessons at home. They don't teach the eucharistic sign so much as they *are* the eucharistic sign to their children. It is from their own bodies that these children have sprung. It is their spirit of love, to whatever extent it exists, which breathes life into these children. It is from their hands that these children receive the manna, the daily bread.

What influence will the developing theology of ministry have on children's liturgy? Perhaps, during the 1980s, religious educators, priests, and other professional religious persons will discover that ministry means leadership. Many questions regarding the eucharistic experiences of children will and must be raised during the next decade; we have hardly touched the surface. The community must sift through them prayerfully and reasonably, select the most important issues, thinking them through together, and then arrive at some definition or action. This is not an impossible task, with gifted leaders facilitating the process—not appropriating it to themselves, but facilitating the reflections of the whole body!

If this comes to pass, then perhaps our harvest will be a hundredfold, after all!

NOTE

1. I recommend that all who wish to form some opinion on this matter read: *Made, not Born: New Perspectives on Christian Initiation and the Catechumenate* (Notre Dame: Murphy Center for Liturgical Research, University of Notre Dame Press, 1976); Eugene Brand, "Baptism and Communion of Infants: A Lutheran View," *Worship* 50 (1976): 29–42; Robert W. Jenson, "The Eucharist: For Infants?" *Living Worship* 15.6 (1979): 1–4; and John Roberto, "Giving Direction to Confirmation," *Living Worship* 15.5 (1979): 1–4.

5

"Taste and See":
Orthodox Children at Worship
Constance Tarasar

> "Do thou, O Master . . . bless also unto every good deed this infant which has been brought here . . . and grant that having been made worthy of Holy Baptism, he (she) may receive the portion of the elect ones of thy Kingdom . . ."
>
> *Prayer for the Child on the Fortieth Day*

Worship in the Orthodox Church is the integrating act by which life is given, sustained, unified, and celebrated. In Baptism, one is born into the new life in Christ; through the seal of the Spirit received in Holy Chrismation, one's personal vocation in that life is confirmed; and in the Eucharist, the newly baptized and confirmed Christian is fully integrated as a member of the Body of Christ to be nourished and sustained by communion with it. These three unique acts are celebrated and received in the liturgy of Christian Initiation. For the vast majority of Orthodox Christians, this threefold sacramental act takes place a few weeks or months after one's birth. The "portion of the elect ones" is generally received by persons who are "children" both in years and in spirit.

The paradox of Christian life is that childhood is seen by Christ as a means to the kingdom, the sign of spiritual maturity: ". . . unless you turn and become like children, you will never enter the kingdom of heaven. Whoever humbles himself like this child, he is the greatest in the kingdom of heaven." (Mt. 18:2) But how can such a view of spiritual maturity be reconciled with the words of St. Paul, who says: "When I was a child, I spoke like a child, I reasoned like a child; when I became a man, I gave up childish ways." (1 Cor. 13:11) And he exhorts us to "attain to the unity of the faith and of the knowledge of the Son of God, to mature manhood, to the measure of the stature of the fulness of Christ; so that we may no longer be children, tossed to and fro and carried about with every kind of doctrine, by the cunning of men, by their craftiness in deceitful wiles." (Eph. 4:13–14)

Childhood and mature humanity in Christ—what do they have in common? Unless we understand their relationship, we cannot understand the nature of spiritual growth, to which both Christ and St. Paul refer, nor can we understand the nature of membership and participation in the Church. The particular place of children in the Church, and especially in her worship, is inextricably tied to our conception of spiritual maturity, church membership, and our understanding of worship itself.

The Human as the Worshipper

Worship is at the center of our life in the Church, for the human person at heart is *homo adorans*, a worshipping being, an adorer and giver of beauty of God and the universe. As such, says Alexander Schmemann, the human person is by definition priest of creation:

> He stands in the center of the world and unifies it in his act of blessing God, of both receiving the world from God and offering it to God—and by filling the world with this eucharist, he transforms his life, the one that he receives from the world, into life in God, into communion with Him. The world was created as the "matter," the material of one all-embracing eucharist, and man was created as the priest of this cosmic sacrament.[1]

Worship is the particular vocation of all Christians, for it is through worship that the unity of the Church and the universe is realized in Christ. No person is barred from that unity for reasons of age, sex, race, or any human division. On the contrary, it is because of human division through sin that humanity has lost the understanding that one's true vocation is to unify in oneself and to adore and to offer to God all that has been received from God.

Children are especially well-suited to this vocation of worshipper, for it is the nature of children to seek to make sense of their world by drawing together the disparate pieces of their environment into some coherent whole. Children have no other vocation: their "work" in the world is to labor to understand it and to unify it in order to use it in a way befitting its nature. For children, the world is not a fragmented world, broken into compartments and categories. Rather, children and their world are inseparable; it is part of them as they are part of it. All the world belongs to children, all the toys are his toys, all food his food, all flowers his flowers, etc.

For good reason the word "mine" is one of the child's first and most frequently used vocabulary words. We must take care not to impose adult norms or judgments on children by thinking them "selfish" in assuming this world into themselves. The child's natural egocentrism in early life cannot be labeled in the negative; for in the context of *homo adorans,* such egocentrism has also a positive value. The whole world belongs to the child, it is the child's to give and to share—which the child freely and often does. If, as adults, we understand that the world truly belongs only to God but is freely given in its entirety to each and all of us to use according to the purposes God intends, we would indeed treat that world and one another in a much more charitable way.

Soon the child learn that the world does not belong solely to any one individual. Each person in the world claims a territory, possessions, even thoughts and values as their own. Competition, aggressiveness, and selfishness become acquired patterns of behavior in order to protect what one has. The patterns of sin, that is, division and separation, are quickly learned; and children are no longer the innocent ones who seek to unify all things in themselves but seek rather to possess all things for themselves. The spiritual dilemma of the child is the dilemma of every person born into "this world."

And this spiritual condition is as certain as is our birth in the flesh. It is the "old man" in us—the "man" separated from God, out of communion with God—that seeks to possess the world for himself, and, in so doing, enslaves both himself and the world. For this reason, Christ comes to free us from our slavery to sin, and to this world that our faith "might not rest in the wisdom of men, but in the power of God . . ." As St. Paul reminds us, "Now we have received not the spirit of the world, but the Spirit which is from God, that we might understand the gifts bestowed on us by God. And we impart this in words not taught by human wisdom, but taught by the Spirit, interpreting spiritual truths to those who possess the Spirit." (1 Cor. 2:5, 12–13)

Both the child and the adult are in need of spiritual transformation. The child needs the cleansing of the new birth of Baptism into the Body of Christ. For the child too must put off the "old nature" which is corrupt, and "be renewed" in the spirit of (his) mind, and put on the new nature, created after the likeness of God in true righteousness and holiness." (Eph. 2:22–24) The child needs the sustenance and nurture of the Body, given in Holy Communion, that one may, with us, "grow up in every way into him who is the head, into Christ, from whom the whole body, joined and knit together by every joint with which it is supplied, when each part is working properly, makes bodily growth and upbuilds itself in love." (Eph. 4:15–16) The Church is supplied with both children and adults who actively participate and contribute to the growth and upbuilding of the Body of Christ.

"Become like children . . .

The nature of childhood is the focus of the relationship of Christ's admonition and St. Paul's understanding of spiritual maturity. Although children are a product of the "old nature" and bear the effects of sin, they exhibit some "signs" which reflect, though imperfectly and in need of transformation, the signs of true spiritual maturity. Three characteristics come to mind: (1) children's total condition of dependency, and the resulting trust that each develops in relations with others; (2) children's ability to learn from the behavior of others, through imitation and modeling; and (3) children's ability to greet the world with an enthusiasm of love and joy. These characteristics of childhood are the central "signs" Christ points to when singling out children as examples of those able to enter the kingdom of heaven. These "signs," when nurtured and transformed by the "new Man" in Christ can become the reality of "mature manhood to the measure of the stature of the fulness of Christ."

Trust and Dependency

Trust and dependency are vital to the child's capacity for growth and development. The infant is totally dependent upon the mother for the satisfaction of personal needs and for the development of the sense of trust that allows for physical and mental growth. At the same time, the mother is dependent upon her child; the child's needs demand an almost slavish and total dedication to the fulfillment of the basic human wants: food, clothing, relief of discomfort, health, and hygiene, as well as the love that allows the child to gain the anticipation and trust that these needs will be met. This physical and emotional dependence upon parents and other adults continues for many years, long after the child has learned to assert personal independence. During adolescence the struggle to become free of dependence intensifies; the parents, also caught in the struggle, realize that even their desire to grant freedom to the emerging adult is tempered by their knowledge that one can't quite "make it on one's own" in today's world. Dependency, therefore, is nearly always viewed as slavery; whether it is due to necessity, convenience, or fear (generally caused by lack of trust) of "going it alone."

For most people, adulthood is realized when the shackles of dependency are thrown off. But are they? Even the jobs at which we work are dependent upon the people and companies who make those jobs possible. Feelings of dependence continue in human relations, be it on the job or in the home. Often, it is now the elder parent who depends on the child for basic needs, and the child is caught in the necessity of providing them. The cycle of dependency seems endless.

Christ's coming has set us free from all forms of slavery to sin, including the slavery of dependence. Yet his very words imply another kind of dependence—a complete and total dependence upon God: "Do not be anxious, saying, 'What shall we eat?' or 'What shall we wear?' For the Gentiles seek all these things; and your heavenly Father knows that you need them all. But seek first his Kingdom and his righteousness, and all these things shall be yours as well." (Mt. 6:31–33) In several places in the gospel, Christ exhorts us to leave all of our earthly possessions in order to follow him. He exhorts us to put our faith and trust solely in God: "If you would be perfect, go, sell what you possess and give to the poor, and you will have treasure in heaven; and come, follow me." (Mt. 20:21)

The initial dependence and trust of the child is without constraints. The child has no fear that its needs will not be fulfilled; such a possibility has not yet been discerned. As the child's wants are supplied, a naive trust develops that assures continual satisfaction whenever these needs arise. Is not this trust and dependence the kind of dependence and trust that Christ wants us to place in God? The difference is that as spiritually mature Christians who know the dangers we face in giving up our "independence" in this world, we freely choose to place our trust and hope in God. We know and believe that God will grant us what is essential for our life. Such faith and trust in God is a daring and bold act of free will: this is an act of humility, not the slave's act of submission or subjugation.

The faith and trust we have in God enables us to place new trust in our fellow human beings. The Epistles of St. Paul are filled with exhortations to mutual dependence: acts freely given and received, fulfillment of one another's needs in love and respect, and a new understanding of obedience and commitment to one another which changes the very character of dependency. Love is the key to this new sense of trust and dependency, for it is love that sets one free to give one's life, willingly and without constraint, for the other. This is the character of childhood that can be transformed into the wisdom of mature humanity in Christ.

Growth through Imitation

Physical, cognitive, and affective development are influenced to a greater or lesser degree by social experience. Simple and complex physical tasks are learned through observation and practice: by witnessing the behavior of others and imitating the actions observed. New ideas and concepts are formed through confrontation with the expressed thoughts of others and the attempt to understand, test, develop, and change those thoughts. Attributes such as honesty, truthfulness, humility, and forgiveness must be witnessed in practice between persons and personally appropriated. Values, morality, and the practice of religion are learned through social encounters and the imitation of models whose beliefs and behavior are valued as examples.

Imitative behavior is not instinctual; it must be learned. It is preceded first by the child's realization that one can intentionally reproduce events (for example, ring a bell, cause an item to fall to the floor, get the attention of mother by a certain behavior). Once the child realizes that one can cause certain effects or events, perception widens and greater attention is paid to the actions of others and the events they cause. Thus, the child seeks to imitate, to reproduce these actions and to build upon them.

"Play" for the child is a way of reproducing and creating realities. Adults can learn a great deal about the child's values by observing play. "Playing house," "church," "school," or "Spiderman" reveals just what and how a child understands and feels about the environment in which one lives and acts. In younger children, there is something sacramental in the character of the child's play. This is serious play; it is more than "pretending," for the child believes for that moment that one is truly representing that person whose character one has "put on." The "props" utilized in play become the reality: the true symbols of the things they represent. An "altar" is built at home out of blocks, or a table is placed in front of the fireplace screen, to serve as the focal point for censing or otherwise imitating the actions of the priest. A father's necktie is transformed into a deacon's stole, an older sister's dress into a vestment, or a pacifier on a string into a censer. The child's imagination enables the transcending of the immediate reality in order to make present another reality. Objects are not "ends" in themselves, but become "means" that can be used to produce new "ends," new realities.

Older children and young adults go beyond the process of imitation when they begin to "model" their lives according to the characteristics and lives of others. The values and behaviors of others are assimilated and provide a basis for the creative development of one's own life. Such imitative and/or modeled behavior can be positive or negative, depending upon how and what one chooses to value. Research indicates that persons tend to model behavior that is rewarded in some positive way and to avoid behavior which is met by punishment or negative consequences. However, in some peer groups, morally negative behavior is encouraged; thus the individual who desires to earn the favor of the group strives to imitate the wrong example. From a Christian perspective, we need to assist children and adults by directing them to models worthy of imitation, such as Jesus Christ and the saints.

The gospels present Christ to us as *The Model*. He is the image of true humanity. Christ himself taught and communicated with others through the modeling process, as he called his disciples to "Come, follow Me!" His obedience, love, and humility served as the example of the teaching he imparted to his followers. He exhorted them to "Let your light so shine before men, that they may see your good works and give glory to your Father who is in heaven." (Mt. 5:16) St. Paul builds upon the concept of Christ as model as he exhorts all to "be imitators of God, as beloved children. And walk in love, as Christ loved us and gave himself up for us, a fragrant offering and sacrifice to God." (Eph. 5:1–2) Christians are advised to imitate St. Paul and the other Christians whose deeds and words have been examples of Christ's life and teaching: "Finally, brethren, whatever is true, whatever is honorable, whatever is just, whatever is pure, whatever is lovely, whatever is gracious, if there is any excellence, if there is anything worthy of praise, think about these things. What you have learned and received and heard and seen in me, do; and the God of peace will be with you." (Phil. 4:8–9)

We must be careful not to misinterpret St. Paul's call as a license for boasting and pride. St. Paul's call to follow Christ was also the call to sacrifice and to abandon one's own will for the sake of the other. Paul accepted this call to love and sacrifice and exhorted others to follow. This call is fraught with danger as a bad example on our part risks the lives of others as well as our own, as Christ warned: "Whoever causes one of these little ones who believe in me to sin, it would be better for him to have a great millstone fastened round his neck and to be drowned in the depth of the sea." (Mt. 18:6)

The call to be imitators of Christ involves a spiritual commitment that is contradictory to that which normally characterizes the modeling process: that is, the desire to imitate those things that are positively valued and rewarded. As the lives of many saints and martyrs illustrate, this call often leads not to positive reward but to negative results: sacrifice, persecution, and death. Not simply acceptance, but transcendence and transformation of the modeling process itself is called for by the gospel. One must be willing to imitate the One who received not praise, but suffering; not the glory of humanity, but the glory of the cross.

Maturation in the Christian life is an eternal process, because it is growth into the likeness of God "from one degree of glory to another." (2 Cor. 3:18) With Christ as the model, the very image of the Father, our vocation as Christians is to make our life one of growth through imitation into the true image and likeness of Christ himself.

Joy and Love

The third characteristic of childhood which reflects the goal of Christian maturity is the presence of love and joy. Children have only one gift to give that is truly their own. Children have no real "possessions," they have only their lives, and the love and joy which those lives can bring to others. Parents have the unique privilege of being the recipients of the child's love and joy which is expressed freely and without limitation. A warm hug, a delightful giggle, or the child's boundless exuberance at play are all examples of the pure expression of the joy of a child. The child's joy and love as well as the expressions of sadness and anger are ways through which one comes to know the world and to experience it in the depths of one's being.

The child does not approach the world rationally; explanations cannot wipe away the hurt of a wound, the absence of an expected gift, the fear that a loved one will not return. Yet, in a moment, tears of sadness can become cries of joy as one's attention shifts to another reality. The child's knowledge is that of present realities, fully experienced as sadness or joy, anger or love, intense concentration or wild abandonment.

The child and the creative genius have something in common: each gives itself up entirely with the totality of its being to the task of solving the problem, searching for the answer or searching for knowledge. The body, mind, and emotion are caught up in one all-consuming effort to the exclusion of all other interests to produce the answer or to find the way. And when that way is found or that key is discovered, the total being explodes in joy. That joy becomes worship, the desire to offer up all that one is and all that one has discovered to the whole world, to anyone who will look or listen, that is, to God.

The sin of the modern world is that one is taught to be "objective" in one's search for knowledge: to be "rational," impersonal, and unemotional. To be truly "objective," one must divorce the mind from emotion, the mind from the senses, and the mind from the body. But then, one must ask: What does it mean to be human? The human person cannot be reduced to mind alone, any more than knowledge, true knowledge, can be reduced to numbers, or people to statistics. Knowledge is subjective because knowledge is personal. The ability to discern is a spiritual gift given by God; it is the mind of Christ which is communicated to us through the person of Christ, who enlightens all humanity in the Spirit. (1 Cor. 2)

In the scriptures, knowledge and wisdom are intimately related to goodness, righteousness, and love. As St. Paul states, the attainment of the higher gifts is achieved in a more excellent way: "If I speak in the tongues of men and of angels, but have not love, I am a noisy gong or a clanging cymbal. And if I have prophetic powers, and understand all mysteries and all knowledge, and if I have all faith, so as to remove mountains, but have not love, I am nothing . . . Love never ends; as for prophecies, they will pass away; as for tongues, they will cease; as for knowledge, it will pass away . . . when the perfect comes, the imperfect will pass away . . ." (1 Cor. 13)

True knowledge is knowledge of God, and God is love. Knowledge and love are inseparable. Love enables one to sacrifice, to give oneself up entirely to the other or to the task at hand. The search for truth and knowledge involves a commitment of the total person: mind, heart, will, and body. One only needs to observe a child who is totally involved in "work," to know what total dedication and love in the search for knowledge is all about. The one who applies this dedication to the search for God is the one who achieves true knowledge, true love and true joy.

The Child as Church Member

This rather lengthy "preface" is necessary for a serious consideration that children are full members of the Church and belong to the Church by virtue of their Baptism and Chrismation in the Body of Christ. There can be no "categories" of Church membership—children or adults, men or women, teens or aged. The Church is neither organization nor government; it is not an agency nor a club of like-minded individuals. The Church is a Body composed of many members, each of whom has a special function or gift, a talent which contributes to the upbuilding of the whole body. Each member is necessary to the body; and "to each is given the manifestation of the Spirit for the common good." (1 Cor. 12) As we have seen, the spirit of childhood which is singled out by Christ as a necessary mark of membership in the kingdom of God is best communicated to us by children. The Church is family, and family includes children as full participating members of the household.

Membership in the Body of Christ is communicated through the sacraments of the Church which are given to both children and adults. The sacraments are potentialities to be personally appropriated and fulfilled. The Orthodox Church has never accepted the concept that only an adult can truly receive and appropriate a sacrament because of rational ability. In our fallen state, the ability to accept or reject the gift of God is determined not by one's rational abilities, but by the degree of one's openness to or alienation from God. One need only look around at the members of any congregation to see that there are indeed many children who are more receptive to God and God's Word than there are adults. Will, not age, is the major determining factor in spiritual growth to "mature personhood" in Christ; adulthood is no guarantee of spirituality. Each person, regardless of age, begins in Baptism that process of spiritual growth "from one degree of glory to another." The gift of life in Christ is given in its fullest potential to all; each must fulfill it according to their own ability.

Taste and See

The practice of integrating children into the life of worship in the Orthodox Church is simply one of immersion into the experience of worship. "Taste and see how good is the Lord" (Prov. 34:8). Experience (taste), then understand (see, be illumined)—this is the methodology. Children who are introduced to worship from the time of infancy accept their role in worship naturally; the church is their home, they become familiar with the surroundings of the temple just as easily as the surroundings of their own homes. The members of the parish that the child sees regularly are as known (and sometimes better known) as the members of the extended family; they are aunts, uncles, cousins, and grandparents. Their common participation in the sacramental life of the Church unites them as one family in the Body of Christ.

The child learns to worship through experience from the very first moments in the Church. The child's first "understandings" come through the senses: one sees the flickering candles, the smoke of the incense, and the colorful movements of celebrants in procession; one hears the music of the choir and the chanting of the priests and readers; one kisses icons, the cross, the gospel book; one smells the fragrance of incense; one feels one's head anointed with oil or splashed with water; and one tastes the wine and bread of holy communion. By the age of one year, the child who is regularly participating in worship will recognize the sights, sounds, smells, tastes, and feel of worship. By age two, children will be imitating many of the things seen and heard: children may imitate the priest censing or carrying the gospel book, the choir director directing the choir. Children will try to make the sign of the cross and will know that the first thing one does upon entering is to kiss the icon or light a candle. A favorite song may be "Alleluia" or "Lord, have mercy." Children especially look forward to receiving holy communion. The child of three or four now looks for the "new" or occasional things that happen in Church: a baptism, the visit of a bishop, the blessing of fruit or palms, or a special feast day.

It is not unusual to hear from a three-year old on such occasions (as at a baptism in our Chapel when the priest lifted a screaming infant out of the water) the question: "Now what's he going to do to her?" What is important for children of this age is that their questions be answered, that they receive "coaching" about "what's coming next," and that they be prepared at home and in church school for the special events or feast days that are approaching. This is what builds the sense of anticipation, the desire to "come and see," and the feeling that one is truly a participant in the common action that is taking place. Children should be in a position where they can see the actions of the celebrants or the choir, rather than the legs of the adult standing in front of them. Though parents may be uneasy about taking their child to the front of the church, it is only there that the child has any real chance of utilizing all the senses to begin assimilating and understanding the nature of worship.

As children grow older, the "Ordo" of the liturgy becomes a source of interest and a key to understanding and following the liturgical celebration. Children who have begun to read enjoy their participation if they can follow parts of the service in a book; the repetition of both hearing and seeing the words helps them to identify the major actions of the liturgy; to discover for themselves "how long is it before communion?" and, gradually, to note changes that occur on special feast days. These understandings can be reinforced if participation in a children's choir (or the regular choir) involves more than learning words or notes at a rehearsal; some explanation of the words or the reason why they are being sung at a particular time can help to enlarge one's concept of worship. The best way to develop an understanding and appreciation of the services is by regular participation.

Not long ago, I visited a children's camp where Vespers and Matins were celebrated daily and the Eucharist twice a week. As I walked into the chapel, a seven-year-old girl recognized me as a visitor and handed me a book of music for Vespers. Several seconds ahead of each section of the service, she turned around to point out the place where I should turn next in the book. She knew the service perfectly! I asked the camp staff how long she had been at the camp and was told that this was the beginning of her second week! To children who have had that experience, it is not unusual to hear them talking about how many "stikhera" we will sing today, or which "Theotokion," or whether or not tonight's service has a full Kanon or the shorter "Triodion" of three odes. Liturgy is enjoyable and interesting, not a strange and boring rite, but a familiar and necessary part of life for a child.

There are two basic reasons that ground the interest and willingness of children to participate in worship: (1) that children naturally worship, and (2) that they have a sense of belonging. The child's play is already a form of worship, a way of creating or recreating reality. Worship understood as the entering into of another reality, the reality of the kingdom, is something the child can readily resonate with, perhaps more readily than the adult. When the child is told that one goes to church to meet God and that the church is God's house, the child accepts and believes. To the child the church *is* God, as is everything associated with the church: the priest, icons, Holy Communion, etc. The child has a sense of the numinous, the holy; and play at home reveals this (e.g. any child who plays "church" inevitably selects a special place for this kind of play, a place that is made "sacred"). The child is *homo adorans*.

The sense of belonging enables the child's inclination for worship to grow and develop. The child responds positively to situations which result in feelings of security, acceptance, and respect as a person. Respect for the child enables the adult to tolerate a certain degree of inattention and listlessness. By that same respect, the adult helps the child to understand and participate more fully. The response of the child's "extended family" in the Church may be even more important than the efforts of the immediate family in making the child feel at home in the Church. Do the adults talk to the children in the Church community? Do they know their names? Do they greet them as they would greet other adults? Do they entrust them with any responsibility? Children must have the opportunity to function side by side with adults in the worshipping community if they are to realize their gifts as members of the Body. Shunting them off to special "children's services" only serves to tell them that they do not belong.

Such actions may seem insignificant, but I am convinced that it is the attitude and nature of the life of the Church community that is responsible for the decision of both children and adults to remain as members of the community or to leave. The life of the Body is critical, for "if one member suffers, all suffer together; if one member is honored, all rejoice together" (1 Cor. 12:26). We know that we are truly members of the Body of Christ not because we have been voted in, or have taken an oath, but because the quality of relationships in that Body tell us that we are truly new members of a new creation, that together we "are no longer strangers and sojourners, but . . . fellow citizens with the saints and members of the household of God, built upon the foundation of the apostles and prophets, Christ Jesus Himself being the cornerstone, in whom the whole structure is joined together and grows into a holy temple in the Lord . . ." (Eph. 2:19–21).

We are all children of worship. We all need to place our trust and faith in Christ, to acknowledge our total dependence upon him for our every breath; to become imitators of his life; and to offer him in full knowledge our joy and love with our entire being. Whether child or adult, we must become like children in spirit, and offer our whole life and whole heart to Christ our God. That is the essence of worship.

NOTE

1. Alexander Schmemann, *For the Life of the World: Sacraments and Orthodoxy* (Crestwood, N.Y.: St. Valdimir's Seminary Press, 1973), p. 15.

6

Children and Worship
Louis Weil

A large number of Episcopal parishes across the country include in their weekly Sunday schedule a "Family Eucharist." In many places this service is the best attended. Yet is this title correct? Is the designation *Family Eucharist* accurate? In my own experience, most of these celebrations are really *adult* liturgies at which children are included for all or part of the service. The mere presence of children does not assure an authentic family liturgy, and the evidence indicates that corporate prayer (including its primary expression in the Sunday Eucharist) is conceived as something basically verbal and cerebral. Until the Church deals with that deeply mistaken view, the title "Family Eucharist" will continue to be a lie.

The worship of the Church is the prayer-action of all its baptized members, Sunday after Sunday: children, women and men; laity and clergy; "high and low, rich and poor, one with another." It is a common offering of praise and thanksgiving to God, through Jesus in the living power of the Holy Spirit. This united action draws together the marvelous diversity of the People of God. In this perspective, children are not a nuisance to be tolerated (or exiled to church school); they are a necessary part of this varied human family. And if they are a necessary part, then it is not so that they may be locked into the rigidities of worship as it is generally conceived. Children must be permitted to bring their own unique perceptions, their spirit, their simplicity and directness into the Christian family's celebration of God's presence in Christ and the Spirit.

The question being posed is not an isolated problem about how to introduce children to full participation in the liturgy. What is involved is a fundamental issue of Christian self understanding. What does it mean to be the Church? Children, by their human nature and Baptism, are appropriate liturgical participants even in infancy. If they are not, then it is virtually impossible to justify the Church's unbroken tradition of Infant Baptism. In fact, that tradition pleads for full participation by all members of the Body. All the known evidence suggests that the practice of Infant Baptism grew out of the strong significance of the family unit in early Christian society and led immediately to full sacramental membership.

The self-understanding of the Church is manifested in its liturgical celebrations. When we look at early liturgical documents, we find evidence of a quite unself-conscious incorporation of the young. Although it is true that their participation was based upon the faith and practice of the parents, there is a kind of naturalness in their inclusion in the full rites of initiation. What is manifest here is the Church's self-understanding as the People of God, an inclusive family of faith directly linked to the natural structures of the human family.

On the other hand, more recent practice suggests another view: children are treated as pre-liturgical persons. Although we baptize infants, their full participation in the Eucharist (i.e., the reception of the Sacrament) is delayed until some *rational* response, some verbal expression of understanding or faith is forthcoming. We make this rational response (whatever we decide it involves) an essential prerequisite for full sacramental participation in the Christian life. In so emphasizing this rational response, we elevate that aspect of the human person out of all proportion to other aspects of personality, including the affective and intuitive powers which children manifest at an early age.

In this regard, children are not the only victims. The emphasis upon the primacy of a rational response is integral to the liturgical mentality which has dominated the Church's prayer for several centuries. Although it is not appropriate to explore that issue in this essay, it is important at least for us to note the very gradual victory of verbalism over all other aspects of liturgical celebration. Not wishing to oversimplify a complex question, I would note the tradition of spontaneous prayer based upon common patterns which the early Church inherited from Judaism. The idea of fixed texts certainly did not develop immediately, but concerns for orthodoxy and control led to an increasing insistence upon verbal conformity. Eventually sacramental validity came to rest in part upon a rigid fixity of text, and the invention of printing permitted a universalization of that rigidity which could not otherwise have occurred.

What we see in this development is the virtual swallowing up through verbal preoccupations of all the other dynamics of liturgical celebration. This emphasis upon the liturgical text carries with it an implied emphasis upon the rational, upon intellectual understanding. Affective and intuitive powers are left with little, if any, space for realization within the liturgical context. Not surprisingly, this emphasis, plus clerical domination of the liturgy, led the development of the liturgy along the path of sacramental minimalism to a preoccupation with an almost mechanistic approach to sacramental meaning.

The authentic inclusion of children in the normative models of parish liturgy may work for the salvation of the adults—and certainly for their wholeness as worshipers. For centuries a false liturgical mentality has tried to let us forget that we have bodies, that we are physical persons, and that our worship involves us with each other—and not merely in perfectly ordered, cerebral ways. We need to learn and live the meaning of Tertullian's phrase, "the flesh is the hinge of salvation." Children bring a naturalness to the liturgy which stands as a judgment upon our overformalized routines. Until they are pressed into behavioral molds, they bring a wonderful openness to the experience of word and gesture, touch and movement—to the whole array of human elements which lie at the heart of the liturgical act. Their feelings find articulation in the corporate context, since they have not learned to put on a religious mask.

From the human side, this whole range of participation rests only in minimal ways upon words and rational understanding. Are we therefore to say that the child's participation is meaningless? Is a person not *capable* of receiving God's gifts until rational understanding is reached? If so, why do we baptize infants? Is the criticism of our Baptist brethren valid? Or is it that we have in our pastoral norms lost touch with what the tradition of Infant Baptism means? Isn't the newborn child *really* a member of the human family? If so, can we not see that the newly baptized child is *really* a member of the Christian family?

The sacraments are first actions on God's part, signs of the presence of the Holy One in our lives. Their meaning does not depend upon our reason. First we are called to *experience* the reality of God's presence. Later there will be ample time to attempt our inadequate verbal descriptions. Children, especially in their pre-verbal openness to an experience, do not analyze, categorize, and define: children receive. "Unless you become as little children, you shall not inherit the kingdom of God." Is this perhaps what Jesus was talking about?

Our consistent liturgical practice in the baptism of infants challenges us to live its implications at the practical/pastoral level, with all the difficulties that may involve. We must begin by recognizing the anomaly of our custom of baptizing infants and immediately denying them the Eucharist. Having Baptism take place at a Family Eucharist at which the newly-baptized do not receive the Sacrament only intensifies the anomaly. Surely the absurdity of this juxtaposition must soon lead us to see that the justification of Infant Baptism rests upon the premises which also justify Infant Communion.

Yet the participation of children in the liturgy is not merely a question of their reception of the Eucharist. Nor is that participation of concern only to parents, as though it were merely the religious dimension of family life. The importance of the participation of children reaches to a still deeper level. Christian worship concerns the whole Christian family, the full membership of the Church. Although the presence of children worshipping with their parents is important, that presence is also important for single persons, for the elderly, and for all who make up the parish community. Children have an integral place in worship which bears significance for the corporate prayer of the whole Church. When that significance is understood, it will require a revolution in our patterns of Sunday worship.

For many centuries Christian liturgy has been conceived as a set of verbal forms authorized from on high, a type of religious drill performed "out there" by authorized persons (the clergy) for passive observers (the laity). But what if we might develop the sense of liturgy as the faith-actions of the local community? In this latter view—which respects and integrates the wonderful diversity of each particular community—all members are active participants, including the children.

Liturgy as faith-actions of the Christian community is not a drill delegated to clerical specialists, but rather that marvelous meeting point of the whole community both to celebrate its faith and at the same time to have that faith nourished by word and sacrament. In this light, the *experience* of liturgy (of which we spoke earlier) becomes far more significant than merely verbal explanations about the liturgy. Children are not excluded because they do not yet understand; they participate—they experience—and later will develop their rational understanding.

Interestingly enough, this is precisely the pattern which the first several centuries of the Church followed with both adults and children. The mystery of God's action in Baptism and Eucharist was first experienced, and only then was explanation given. For centuries we have turned this order around in our pattern of Christian formation, and the results are disastrous. Liturgy has ceased to be the *natural* activity of the Christian, but rather a quite peculiar set of religious customs performed on Sundays, or occasionally, or for many not at all. Our contemporary situation requires the common sense which we see at work in the pattern of the early centuries. Although it would be foolish to attempt to take over the early pattern as a strict model, since our cultural situation is so radically different, we can adapt its insights to our own context. In the classical initiatory pattern, there was no rush either to Baptism or Eucharist. The candidates passed through a long period of socialization during which an organic process of the assimilation of Christian values might take place. The liturgy, when at last it was experienced, was the ritual expression of that whole organic development. The impact of the signs was not merely in their dramatic enactment but more radically in their articulation of the experience of conversion.

When liturgy is apprehended first through experience, the appropriateness of the full participation of children is evident. Children experience much that they cannot verbally articulate. We do not delay the first bath until the child understands hygiene, nor do we require knowledge of nutrition prior to the first meal. The child experiences many baths and many meals—really experiences them—and at the most basic human (and preverbal) level, apprehends their meaning through the experience.

Similarly, children experience in the liturgy human actions into which they enter in day-to-day life as members of a family: greeting, embracing, gathering with the family, listening to a good story, asking forgiveness, saying "thank you," washing, eating, celebrating. Yet how often these direct parallels between daily life and Christian worship are suffocated by our prepackaged approach to liturgy. The liturgical experience of children is formative. If the underlying human gestures of the liturgy are minimalized through excessive formalization, the child will *learn* (in the deepest, formative sense) that Christian faith is alien to human life, a separate religious category which is not directly related to the fabric of day-to-day living.

Attitudes toward family, the table, and sharing a meal are learned through constant experience in the home. If the eating of a meal is normally a private matter of meeting a physical need, or if the gathering of the family is not experienced as a joyful expression of a common life, how can we ever expect the obvious parallels with the Sunday Eucharist to be realized and bear fruit? The best family liturgy on Sunday morning cannot alone convey to children the meaning of Christian life and prayer. It should be learned at home. But one would be naive not to know the embarrassment such a suggestion provokes. Regular family prayer is rare, and I am convinced this is precisely because, for the greater majority even of practicing Christians, both corporate and private prayer is seen as something apart from real life. One only has to be asked to watch a child "say his prayers" to realize how artificial it is even in homes where the effort is made. Yet if we once know the simple joy of sharing in the prayer of a family that prays as part of its daily life, we experience the depth of its importance. As long as prayer is absent or artificialized in the home, there is little hope that Sunday worship can be other than a foreign intrusion, a religious routine of no real meaning in life.

The full incorporation of children into our corporate prayer will require an enormous change of mentality on the part of the Church at large. It will elicit a deeper sensitivity to the nonverbal dimensions of worship. It will require an end to stuffy formality. Best of all, it will help us discover the naturalness of Christian prayer.

Part Two

PRACTICE

7

The Rite of Anointing and the Pastoral Care of Sick Children
Jerome W. Berryman

I n recent years, the Rite of Anointing has been reestablished as a pastoral tool for ministry to the sick.[1] The contemporary renewal of this rite focuses on the sick person with flexibility in considering the needs of those who surround the sick person.

The rite's central mystery is the renewal of relationships broken by illness and/or approaching death. This liturgical act expresses the reunion of the sick with their self-concept of health/wholeness. The isolated sick person is reunited with the community of faith who are joined in a deeper relationship with God. When these three relationships are healed, through the act of anointing, healing is enhanced. Understanding the "healing" operation of the Rite of Anointing, we must consider the special needs of sick children.

How Children Make Meaning

Meaning is made in relationships. It is an orientation in the inner and outer world. Meaning is one's relationship to reality and becomes reality by our faith in it, since our participation makes it real. This is a circle of reasoning, but it is also the way human beings make meaning in an on-going, self-adjusting way.

The fiduciary character of all knowledge and discovery was one of Michael Polanyi's main theses.[2] He broke the circle of reasoning and joined the dilemma of "faithing" to know or knowing to have faith into a process of creation. Polanyi was a scientist who realized that science was not purely objective. He disputed the idea that science was impersonal and only uncovered facts. He argued that all knowledge was personal and that it was a disservice to abdicate this responsibility in any field from the study of crystals to that of economics.

The knower and the known are a relationship of participation in each other. To know through fiduciary relationships is what I mean by "making meaning." It is my intent to identify reality in the relationship rather than in any part of the relationship-network's points of reference.

To discover how a child makes meaning we need to look at four aspects of this process of being-in-relationships: the stages of faith development; the lifestyles of these stages; the process of change (or the destruction of meaning); and the language appropriate for meaning in faith relationships.

The structures of faith are grounded in the earliest of experience before the infant makes distinctions among self, human, less-than-human, and more-than-human. This time is pre-verbal, pre-conceptual, and prior to the development of "thought" processes. Erik Erikson has described this time as the period when we work out the basic building blocks of future development. Will we trust or not?[3] An optimal resolution of this question emerges as hope.

For purposes of analysis, I will separate faith's presence into the four kinds of structures: stage; style; process; and language. This division of the faith system prepares us to enable people to be themselves. It also enhances our ability to communicate with people unlike ourselves, such as children.

Faith Stages

James W. Fowler has developed a theory of stages of faith.[4] He identifies six levels of faith with an analysis of seven variables: relationship to nature; relationship to society and ethics; perspective-taking ability; relationship to authority; social reference; use of symbol system; and relationship to symbols. The naming of a stage of faith is an indication of its interpretation. Therefore, I will discuss Fowler's faith stages in my own terminology.

There is a silent stage before verbal communication. This is the time that infant and mother may communicate through a consistent set of signs and sounds that serves as a language for them but not for the society. Once children enter the linguistic world of their society, a researcher can begin to analyze the logic structures each child uses to relate to reality by a faith development interview.

Stage One is the time of the *natural but naive theologian:* the optimum way to relate to reality is by an I-Thou relationship with all of life, including God. Gradually a semantic separation from the small child's involvement with the global experience of life begins to develop. The world begins to take shape as it is named by verbal bits and pieces. By the time children enter school, they have become so involved in this semantic world that another way of "faithing" develops. A new logic begins to assert itself as a whole for the faith relationship with reality.

Stage Two is that of the *natural but naive empiricist:* empirical fact replaces fantasy as the optimum focus for knowing reality and relationship to it. Language begins to separate itself from what it names, so that the child gains more control over it. Symbols become less magical (numinous and identical with what they name) and become mythic and literal signs for facts. All of life is tied together into a narrative which gives it coherence. The stories of sacred traditions are a mythic-literal way to make meaning. A second level of language allows the child to step back from total immersion.

Stage Two is a time when fantasy seems naive. It is replaced by a new optimum way of relating: the classification and grouping of the names of people and things. Words remain literal and tied to things but not in so magical and numinous a way as during the pre-school years. Each stage gives away some of the exclusive intensity of the previous stage's ability in exchange for a new ability. The old stage seems naive while the new "optimum" ability seems to be the most powerful form of relationship one could have.

Stage Three is that of the *natural but naive logician:* language finds both fantasy and narrative as naive ways to put the world together. It gives one an ability to think about thinking or story or fantasy. Levels in the mythic narratives of religious traditions are enjoyed, and the power of logic over nature begins to be fully appreciated.

By this time of development, logic is more independent of concrete involvement with actual persons and things. Parts of an experience can be held in suspension while there is speculation about what would happen if only one variable were investigated. A hypothesis can be made and tested against the empirical facts. The design of a scientific experiment requires such a relationship with reality. Scientists might work very well in a lab under another's direction and live within the mythic-literal understanding of science, but leadership in this form of knowing requires a Stage-Three relationship with reality. There is a similarity to Piaget's stage of formal operations. Fowler's Stage Three extends this beyond the values of the scientific tradition into the values of the tradition of Western religion.

Stage Four is that of the *natural but naive de-mythologizer:* a major step which requires each individual to take ownership for an individual worldview. It goes beyond citing authorities to being one's own authority. This development requires time and experience. Occasionally, a few people in their thirties begin to suspect that life is more than an analysis of the concepts of anthropology, sociology, psychology, biology, and all the other "ologies." These do not provide an adequate approach to making meaning and they exclude other levels in one's channels of communication in relationships. Once the self is de-mythologized and is seen as relative to other people, the individual has begun the shift into the next stage.

Stage Five is that of the *natural but naive re-mythologizer:* the individual considers conceptual analysis to be naive. There is a realization of the many levels of communication for relationships with ultimate reality. For example, an analysis of Holy Communion may be interesting and instructive, but it may separate you from experiencing reality in that special way. There is a conscious shift of meaning to know in a way that you did as a child. What you rejected at an earlier time, you re-appropriate for nourishment at this time.

Stage Six is that of the *non-naive theologian:* it is a quiet time which communicates on many levels simultaneously. This person is aware of these different levels of communication and that awareness is of great importance. An individual may discover this awareness by the early forties; but few people become non-naive about faith relationships. This stage is the paradoxical culmination that has emerged through this development. This is a time which is simultaneously the most centered and the most open. Ego-striving has ceased. The depth and multi-leveled range of relationship with reality of this stage relinquishes the need for metaphors and symbols. This individual may have become a metaphor or symbol for other persons. Jesus of Nazareth may have been in the transformation from Stage Five into Stage Six when he stopped telling parables. He realized that he had to become a parable. Even as the parable, he was still a child who called out to his father on the cross. The faith of a Stage-Six individual is like the pre-stage faith experience, except that the naivete is gone.

Faith Style

What I call faith "style" originally was articulated by Paul Tillich.[5] His approach, reminiscent of C. G. Jung, was to distinguish between inward-tending and outward-tending styles of faith. Inward-tending faith was onto-logical and outward-tending faith was moral.

Tillich identified four forms of inward-tending faith. In the sacramental form of faith, ultimate reality is experienced in a piece of general reality such as bread, wine, or water. The second form of inward-tending faith is mystical and the ultimate is experienced by overcoming the distance between the knower and the known. The third form of inward-tending faith does not use religious language but experiences the ultimate in nature. The fourth form of inward-tending faith is also without religious language as it experiences the ultimate in human history.

Tillich identifies four forms of outward-tending faith styles. First, the ultimate may be experienced in the observance of Divine Law. Second, the ultimate may be experienced in the action of interpreting God's law in each situation reflecting a relationship with God that gives law creative meaning for each new occasion. Third is a form of outward-tending faith that does not use religious language; the ultimate is experienced in action dictated by natural law. Fourth, the ultimate is experienced in action dictated by utopian extensions of human history expressed in secular terms.

er, these layers of meaning cannot be peeled back like an onion or an archeological exploration. They interact in a circle of meaning interdependent of but interrelated in a process of deep understanding. A similar phenomenon is operative in the primary symbols of classical religious. This search for the total but unarticulated experience of the symbols of evil as well as the sacramental symbols of healing is an acknowledgment that these are the two sides of the human biopsychosocial experience.

Evil is physically experienced before it becomes verbalized. The primary symbols such as a cry or a shudder become verbal confessions of defilement, guilt, and sin in ritual and poetry. The myths of the beginning and end of evil are the second level of verbal expression. The third level of symbols is conceptual: the servile will, the philosophy of fault or original sin. There are some irrational roots to the logic of this level of symbolization which grounds the administration of the healing rites. These liturgical acts (e.g., Holy Communion, Baptism, Reconciliation) are the experiences that can engage the biopsychosocial experience of evil by presenting a living experience that balances the emerging articulation of defilement, guilt, and sin.

It is the Rite of Anointing that primarily engages the infection aspect of evil that one experiences as defilement, stain, and blemish from the outside. The subjective burden of this broken bond with the sacred and other defilement is guilt. Holy Communion engages guilt on the most primary level. The ontological bondage and alienation of sin may be engaged and healed by Baptism or through Confirmation, while Marriage and Holy Orders engage the social spectrum of biopsychosocial systems that evil affects. Reconciliation engages all elements of the experience of evil equally. These rites overlap the equivocal experience of evil and are entry points into the global experience. This experience of evil is "equivocal, laden with a multiplicity of meanings."[8]

To reach into that deep region beyond language which promotes fundamental healing, we need the symbols of religious language to undergird the reductionistic language of science. The Rite of Anointing promotes healing through a nonverbal shift from a destructive framework into a constructive framework for the biopsychosocial systems. Whether one is sick or dying, the antidote for evil's defilement is to "re-frame" and create meaning despite its intrusion. This "re-framing" of one's life is possible only with the support and continuity with one's past healthy self as well as with the community of faith and with God. The Rite of Anointing contributes to this grounding at deep levels.

The question becomes how would I approach a child in the hospital to offer this symbolic act for renewal and healing? How is the liturgical art practiced in this act?[9]

The Preliminary Visits

The offering of the Rite of Anointing to any other person is an intimate act. However, when the patient is a child the intimacy of the act intensifies. A relationship with the child must be established beforehand, and is grounded in the understanding and common expectation that the parents have shared with their children.

It is common practice that the hospital chaplain will come to know terminal patients in a more in-depth manner because of the duration and regularity of treatment; for example, chemotherapy for cancer patients. Those who come into the hospital with a broken limb or the need for brief therapy will not have enough time to establish a bond of trust necessary for an optimum offering of the Rite of Anointing.

This case study is derived from the development of a trusting relationship among the chaplain, parents, and child. The level of meaning developed in this relationship allowed for the nonverbal approach to the unspeakable through the Rite. There may be a pre-existent relationship of trust between the parents, child, and chaplain which has grown out of worship or education experiences, or has been established by several visits during the hospital stay. A preliminary approach to gain the parents' permission and support to bless the child may become the foundation for administration of the Rite of Anointing.

The Blessing of the Child

Having gained the parents' permission, the chaplain prepares for the Blessing of the Child. The parents have told the child that something special will happen when the chaplain visits. Prior to entering the child's space, the chaplain should pause and consider personal peacefulness. The chaplain knows that what is felt or expressed non-verbally is as important as the verbal exchange which is about to take place. The awareness of the presence of God's grace and of the child in this sacramental relationship will help heal the chaplain's shortcomings.

Upon entering the room, the chaplain may cross towards the child's bed and greet the parents with an opening phrase from the adult rite, "Peace to this house and to all who live in it." Their response, "The peace of the Lord be with you," indicates their active participation in this sacramental relationship. It is during this time that eye contact with the sick child must be maintained. This signals that although you are there for the child, you also invite the participation of the adults who care for the child.

Despite the previous relationship with the parents and child, the chaplain should slowly engage the child in a typical activity or discussion before a verbal consideration of blessing. After this initial period has passed and the basic relationship with the child has been established, the chaplain might ask the child, "Do you know what a blessing is?" Perhaps the child has seen this in church or has witnessed the custom of blessing the home or other important passage in life. Patience is the critical characteristic of the chaplain who asks the waiting child, "Do you know how a blessing works? May I show you? It works something like this."

The chaplain takes something that has deep personal meaning such as a ring and holds it in an outstretched hand. The object is held between the fingers so the child cannot see it. The object *must* be precious to the chaplain so that the nonverbal communication will agree with the explanation being offered to the child. The chaplain drops the precious object into the waiting open hand below. "When I give you a blessing for God, it is like God giving you a special gift. It sort of falls on you like that ring did. You don't have to do anything. It just happens."

The chaplain places a hand on the child's head once permission to pronounce the blessing has been granted. It is important to say the child's name with deep awareness in the blessing. Saying a child's name during a liturgical act is not a mere formality, it is a significant part of the rite. The verbal blessing should be brief as the chaplain's hands rest on the child's head in silence. Perhaps the adults in the room may be included in the acts of "laying on hands" in silence or with the words of blessings.

Once the liturgical act is accomplished, the chaplain steps back and waits for the experience to settle in. There is more to this experience than words or actions. Depth of meaning is found in and through the relationship. A return to the normal levels of relationship takes time. It is difficult to keep a chronological awareness of time when sacred time has been recognized.

In an effort to make this transition to regular time, the chaplain begins to move away from the child's bed while speaking to the adults in the room or asking the child about a toy or a television show. The chaplain tells the child about tomorrow's visit and is careful not to make vague references about time. Adults too often confuse children when they say "in a minute" or "only a second." It is helpful if the chaplain can relate tomorrow's visit with something the child experiences on a routine basis in the hospital. After a verbal closure of this special visit, the chaplain may indicate a future contact with the parents to reconfirm their support for the Rite of Anointing.

The Anointing of the Child

The day arrives for the Rite of Anointing. The chaplain remembers that the nonverbal language is important and centers the sense of self. Upon entering the child's room, the chaplain carries the case holding the materials for the Rite of Anointing. This engages the child's curiosity as the case projects a certain magic and respect. The case is white symbolizing celebration, such as Christmas or Easter; and ties the Rite of Anointing to the Rite of Baptism.

As the chaplain enters, all present receive greetings but the focus of attention is on the case and the child. This is the primary link. Moving slowly, the chaplain may say, "I have brought you a very special surprise today. I am so glad to be back today with you all. It is especially good to see you again, (Mary)." The chaplain places the case on the child's bed and hopes to raise the child's curiosity about the case.

Once the child's curiosity is aroused, the chaplain is asked about the case. It is opened and the contents are examined and explained to the child. "This is the special bottle. It is very beautiful because there is something precious inside." Each of the anointing materials is identified. The value is expressed nonverbally in the way the chaplain holds these ritual elements. Once this has been completed, the time to share the rite has arrived. "May I put a little of this oil on you for God and all the people in the world who love children? They would like for you to have their good feelings."

If the child gives permission, the chaplain can prepare for the Rite of Anointing. The preparation for the rite is a prayer which results in a centering quiet.

> Thank you, God for this holy Oil,
> filled with good feelings for
> *Mary* (or "this child") who is sick.
> Amen.

The prayer is short, but not done quickly. Every word should be savored and dwelt upon with the child. Clarity of expression and depth of intent are the crucial characteristics for these prayers—they are meant to be real for the child—not confusing or inadequate.

"Now we are ready. I would like to anoint the part of you first that is the most important. This is where the good feelings ought to go first. Where shall I anoint you first?" This gives the child a chance to participate fully in the rite by indicating the most essential part of the ill body. The adult rite assumes the importance of the head and hands. However, the child has different values assigned to parts of the body than an adult's body image. The child's responses to these questions are important not only for the adaptation of the rite to their needs, but also for the health-care team. An understanding of the child's perception of the parts that "feel good" and those that "feel bad" can be useful in determining a more accurate diagnosis for the child's medical care.

Careful attention must be paid to any indication of response to these questions. A gesture, a glance or words might emerge to guide in the first act of anointing. This first act should be the child's; it is also an opportunity for a testing of the chaplain. Many people come to the child's bedside with little rituals which hurt, so the child may still be suspicious despite the chaplain's genuine care.

As the child's most important place is anointed, the chaplain might pray:

> God and all the people who truly love
> children, anoint you now with this oil.
> May it fill you with the good feelings
> so many have for you.
> Amen.

Once the anointing is completed, the chaplain might inquire if there are other important places the child would like to have anointed. Children may feel that this experience should be applied to many important parts of their bodies. If this becomes a manipulative game, re-anoint the first place and conclude.

Children may request the anointing of the place that worries them the most. This "worry-point" might be an incision; a smooth head after chemotherapy; legs that don't work right; a bad-smelling place; or some other place that children's logic has suggested is dangerous to their well-being. If this place is covered by a dressing or cast, anoint the dressing or cast. If it is uncovered, there is no need to worry about medical infection.

Once the "worry-point" is anointed, a prayer might be offered:

> God and all the people who truly love
> children, anoint you now with this oil.
> May it fill you with the good feelings
> so many have for you even in this place
> that worries you.
> Amen.

Each "worry-point" ought to be given equal attention. One is never sure where children's logic will locate the source of pain and worry, so an open mind will allow the child to be a guide in verbal and nonverbal ways to these points of concern. This helps children to re-claim good feelings despite the anxiety these "worry-points" cause.

Once the anointing is completed, the chaplain might gesture for the others present to join with the child for closing prayer:

> Thank you, God, for this child,
> a very special person named *Mary*.
> When *Mary* is afraid, comfort her.
> When she is lonely, be her friend.
> When she is worried, let her speak about it.
> Help *Mary* know that the Oil of Anointing
> is filled with good feelings for her

and that there is no place she goes,
or anything she does, or any way she feels
that can stop them from being with her.
They are hers.

                                        Amen.

With the closing prayer finished, the group may remain quiet until the silent substratum of the prayer concludes. This might be indicated by a verbal, "Amen."

The child should be invited to help put the anointing materials away. This activity helps the child with the transition to regular time and space, to the ordinary channels of communication. It also helps the adults who are present, including the one who has offered the rite, to make the same adjustment.

Before leaving, the chaplain may want to assure the child that one can wash where the Anointing was made. "It cannot be washed away. It might look like it is gone, but you can't wash away good feelings. Don't worry, they will always be there. They are yours now."

Conclusion

My interpretation of the Rite of Anointing is a liberal approach based on the developmental needs of the child. The rite is centered around the act of anointing itself; and this act has been divided into an anointing of the "most important part" of the child as well as the "worry-point." The child's inter-pretation of these places is given primary focus as each individual has a different sense of "bodiliness," and that of a child is not that of an adult.

The basic flow of the adult rite has been maintained, with certain elements smoothed over for a single point of focus. The centrality of this rite is a nonverbal, multi-level experience of evil encountered by a rite to resist evil and to heal the broken relationships. The wholeness of health is broken by disease, but disease also causes us to become more aware of the depths of the indirect, significant liturgical act of anointing. The anti-meaning of evil can be healed when an awareness of death is given a new frame that the sick person is not alone and good feelings extend to wherever we are, whatever we do, and however we feel. We need children to teach us this truth.

There is another form of healing in this discussion. It is a healing of the body of the Church. The Rite of Anointing has not been a major point of disagreement among Eastern, Catholic, and Protestant Christians. Perhaps formal ecumenical agreement can be made concerning a unified Rite for Anointing of Sick Children. What better place to start? These divisions in Christianity do not make sense to children anyway.

NOTES

1. *Rite of Anointing and Pastoral Care of the Sick, Provisional Text* (Collegeville: The Liturgical Press, 1974).
2. Richard Delwick, *The Way of Discovery* (New York: Oxford University Press, 1979). This provides an introduction to Polanyi's thought and relates it to many fields such as science and theology.
3. Erik H. Erikson, *Childhood and Society* (New York: W. W. Norton Co., 1950). In the Revised Edition (1963) please see Chapter Eight, "Stages of Man".
4. James W. Fowler, *Stages of Faith* (New York: Harper & Row, 1981).
5. Paul Tillich, *Dynamics of Faith* (New York: Harper & Row, 1957).
6. James E. Loder, *The Transforming Moment: Understanding Conviction Experiences* (New York: Harper & Row, 1981).
7. Paul Ricoeur, *The Symbolism of Evil* (Boston: Beacon Press, 1976).
8. This description of the administration of the Rite of Anointing to sick children is based on my work at the Learning Lab, Institute of Religion's Children's Center, Texas Medical Center, Houston, Texas.
9. The parts of the adult Rite that have been smoothed over are indicated in the following outline of the rite by "°":

    1. Introduction and Greeting (68)
   °2. Penitential Rite (71)
   °3. Liturgy of the Word (72)
   °4. Litany (73)
   °5. Laying on of the Hands (74)
    6. Blessing (75) or Thanksgiving for the Oil (75b)
    7. Anointing (76)
    8. Prayer (77)
   °9. Lord's Prayer (78)
  °10. Communion if appropriate (55–58)
  °11. Blessing (79)

Assembly
Gabe Huck

To speak of assembly is to focus on those who do the liturgy. Everyone who comes—presider, lector, usher, acolyte and worshipper—is a part of the assembly. What this assembly does is the common prayer of Christians. Rites and documents reflect this priority; for example, the *Rite of Baptism for Children*[1] and *Christian Initiation*[2] speak first of the Church. These documents describe what is going on in this assembly as the gathering up of symbols. What the assembly does is liturgy.

Another document, *Environment and Art in Catholic Worship*, makes it clear that the assembly, these folks that are this local Church, is the environment for whatever is to be done. This document refuses to let us separate the people from the liturgy, and sets the tone for this essay. "Each church gathers regularly to praise and prayer, to realize and celebrate the kingdom of peace and justice. That action of the Christian assembly is liturgy."[3] That's what liturgy is and everything liturgy is: people thanking, remembering, offering prayer, and aware of how wonderful and difficult is the reign of God.

More and more, we hear of the assembly, and regularly it will be listed among the other ministries, but we are far from taking it seriously. Most Sunday morning experiences would never lead one to believe that assembly and action belong in the same breath. At some churches, nothing is done to rouse our sense of praying together; while at others, we are entertained or educated or impressed. Slowly we are beginning to seek out those places where we are expected and allowed to pray.

More and more, we are becoming aware of how many people have a hand in the Sunday liturgy: someone to prepare the building, to read the scriptures, to preside, to greet and seat people, to take the collection, to bake the bread, to buy the wine, to play the organ, to sing, to preach, and to coordinate all this. All of these, except perhaps the bread baker, are members of the local church. They are people who have offered their gift of a good voice, a ready smile, or skill in arranging flowers. Some do their work well, some have their off-days, while others would be better in another role. Yet all of them depend on "somebody" not included on the list.

To call ourselves Christians is to acknowledge the wonderful presence of God. But part of being human is using all the human creaturely things to respond to that presence of God: to praise, thank, petition, and repent. All those roles we named respond with words spoken, bread baked, or music played. It's not God who is needed to take all those different sorts of service and make it prayer, it's *us*.

The Eucharist, or any liturgy of our churches, isn't just like anything else. It is a little like a number of things we humans do. All such things depend not simply on some special people doing their work well. Certainly a birthday party needs a cake baker, candlemaker, and someone having a birthday. A football game requires players, referees, groundskeepers, ticket-takers, and cheerleaders. A family dinner needs cooks, tablesetters, and dishwashers. But all this would fall flat without the folks who really enjoy being there and are anxious to lend their voices, hands, smiles, and hearts.

All those who do something special at Mass depend on *us*. It is as one of us, the assembled Church, that they do their special thing. We can no longer speak of "going to church on Sunday" as if that consisted in just getting one's body into a certain building for a particular period of time, nor of "saying my prayers at Mass" as if the Mass could go on without me. We have often thought of Mass as something to be attended like a lecture, watched like a play, heard like a radio program, or sung like an Arthur Fiedler concert. But we are a ways from knowing Mass as something we *do*.

As people involved with liturgy, we have let our attention bounce from this sacrament to that, from this ministry to that, and from this occasion to that one. That word "regularly" in the statement "Each church gathers *regularly* . . ." is crucial. The steadiness of the week-by-week Sunday prayer of these people depends on the quality of the steady experience. We must remember two important and related ideas: first, that our considerations as planners and ministers must acknowledge that liturgy is the work of the assembly; and second, that we all need the skills and arts for the praising, thanking, remembering, praying, and realizing the kingdom in common that must occur in liturgy.

The Church: Christian Assembly of Praise

The first thing an assembly does is assemble: this involves everything that happens from the car door to the first reading. There are formal and informal moments, but all relate to transition, to the gathering of many lives to do something in common. If things fail here, little can be expected from the rest of the ritual. Every routine arrangement is to be such that it lets us settle into being the assembly; not because we are told to be but because it is so inviting and so natural to be the assembly.

The hospitality of place and people is crucial, and it is difficult. Few gatherings demand that we be hospitable to such a wide variety of human persons: ages, sexes, sizes, and personalities. For the church which holds us together in fath does nothing to change our great differences. What other gatherings make room for the toddler and the grandmother, the teenager and the parents? There are some: the subway, the elevator, the beach, and the baseball park. Subway, elevator, and beach are ways to somewhere else or center on remaining an individual or small group. At the baseball park, at least, we need to join in common sound and gesture.

It is no easy thing to make such a diversity of persons feel "at home." Even when we are at a home, living rooms infrequently feel as welcome to a child as to a teenager as to an adult. And yet there are places whose environment— and people whose manner—is welcoming to all. You may meet it in a library or a park or a bus driver. These are qualities we seek; all of us have met them here and there. We must be careful of thinking that the warm greeting will work wonders by itself. Being comfortable about being with other people to pray is, like so much else at liturgy, a readiness that, if exercised only on Sunday, has little chance to flourish.

Much depends on the seating. We have not convinced people that what they are there to do on Sunday depends on all the understanding and feelings conveyed by sitting together. Most parishes offer Mass at all the various hours. Many times, half the pews are empty. Mass should be offered when the seats can be filled, then no one will sit alone.

On a bus or at a movie, we sit apart. And that cultural model operates in the church. "Move to the front of the church" causes as much reaction as "move to the back of the bus." What's needed is internal motivation: I want to be part of what goes on here. This movement is acknowledged by those who have made time elsewhere for private prayer and know this as the time for public prayer. For these persons, this has become a habit, not a now and then activity. The habit of steadily taking our place to pray beside others is a small but crucial part of the assembly's ministry that can't be separated from how this part of Sunday fits into the whole of Sunday.

There are other more formal elements to these rites of transition moving us together toward community prayer and the right spirit for the scriptures and the Eucharist. There is danger that these rites may do just the opposite: dissipate attention before it is gained. The key question is a way of beginning, of moving gently into the prayer. If a song is used, it is not to get the presider down the aisle nor to entertain. Rather, song lets us hear and sense the presence of others. This is a transition rite of movement towards doing something together. Song serves well in this tradition. A familiar song provides a feeling of "being at home" in this church and creates a sense of community as all the voices merge into one great sound.

The opening prayer is important for the silence that comes prior to the prayer itself. Many people being quiet together and keeping still together conveys a sense of community as strongly as does a well-sung opening hymn. It is the habit that matters, and letting the silence last long enough for the nervousness to go away and for the real quiet to settle. It is also important that the call to prayer spoken by the presider, "Let us pray," be a true invitation. The presider and other ministers mirror the still and silent prayer of the assembly.

Gathering and offering hospitality to one another, singing, joining in the sign of the cross, and keeping a great and prayerful silence: that's how an assembly develops a familiar pattern of initiating prayer. This takes care and skill on the part of the presider, leader of song, and ushers, which enables the assembly to do its gathering.

The liturgy of the word is our weekly rite of storytelling. The steady round of readings from the Lectionary and the special stories of the seasons tell and re-tell the community's story. People who come together, despite so many differences, need regularly to tell the stories that have formed their common bond. The assembly's role is to listen. The Liturgy of the Word works well when the assembly is a good listener. This requires attention to the spoken word, not the printed word. It means that scripture is encountered regularly outside the time of liturgy as well as within it. But most of all, it means that we are convinced that this is our own story.

The Liturgy of the Word is punctuated with times of silence which need to last awhile so that words are not heaped upon other words. Even when well spoken, words have no room to take root unless there is silence. Children and adults can discover here what is denied by our culture: the time for contemplation. We can learn the delights of this, to savor the words and phrases from the scriptures and the homily and to breathe these in and out in the silent time.

The psalm is central to the assembly's prayer. The storytelling ritual asks reflection not only in silence but in the psalms. The psalms find a place at communion, but their special place in all our liturgy is to care for our time of reflection. They flow from our silences and demand no text or hymnbook. Psalms rarely if ever do their work if spoken; they require a special singing which is meditative and repetitive. The Lectionary proposes that there be seasonal refrains and psalms that the assembly might learn by heart and keep from year to year, season to season. Here is a way that the prayer of the weekly Eucharist of the large assembly can enrich the prayer of the individual at home.

The psalms contain a vocabulary of prayer that draws on what is deepest and oldest in our Judaeo-Christian tradition. They contain our finest images for grasping our own condition: praises and curses; belonging and loneliness; struggle and calm. From the psalms should come the prayer we know by heart and use for morning, evening, and table prayers, and for times of joy and sorrow. This happens when the assembly believes that this is prayer that gathers us together, that bears the possibility of all our centuries, and that is capable of the beauty of how we sound together.

Another moment in the Liturgy of the Word which shapes the assembly is the time in this rite when we offer prayers of intercession. Much depends on how we understand this kind of prayer. The most sensible answer is that this is litany. So we look to what makes a litany good ritual: repetition and rhythm are the ways one is engaged in the movement of prayer. The assembly needs to be familiar with the refrain and needs a leader who can establish a steady pace for this prayer. The moment itself is needed to climax the rituals that have surrounded the storytelling. There is no essential relationship which places intercessory prayer at this particular place in the liturgy. Yet these prayers put before us the needs of the world and the church, renew our sense of community in prayer, and remind us that the story we have been telling continues.

After this litany of intercession, there are tasks to be done like the setting of the table and the gathering of money. This is a private time between the two rituals. The gathering of money finds a home in the informal character of this time. One of the important things the assembly does is this collection for the poor and the church. The collection is about a Holy Communion these people envision and make possible.

Within the eucharistic prayer, the vision of the assembly's task is farthest from the reality. The very silent atmosphere of this prayer twenty years ago is often replaced by unfocused attention. For example, the announced responses, the institution narrative turned into a dramatic reading, and the singing of the acclamations to unworthy melodies, work against the assembly's doing the eucharistic prayer. Then there are the problems of posture and the absence of any sensed presence of bread and wine. The familiar prayers sound like monologues with occasional breaks for the people to sing a short song. Greatest of all the problems—and the one which remains when all others are remedied—is our inability to give praise and thanks. We have not learned a way of life that overflows with thanks and praise. So this prayer, which should be one of praise and thanks to God, can do no more than reflect and perhaps inspire the Christian soul.

For now, we can work on little things: an uncluttered table on which the bread and wine can be clearly seen; the strong, direct manner of the presider in the dialog; and the meaningful use of gesture for the acclamations. The document on *Environment and Art* reminds us "Give God thanks with the human means . . ." In the weekly eucharistic prayer we have those human means to evoke all the praise that is in us, to give sound and gesture to our thanksgiving. This is the assembly's task, the climax of our prayer together.

The gestures of the communion rite make clear that the Holy Communion is this people. The Lord's Prayer binds together bread and forgiveness. The gesture of peace gives definition to the eating and drinking which are to follow. There is a meditative litany as the bread is broken which captures what the whole of this gathering means. The invitation is given to all to eat and drink together. How this is done matters greatly. Ministers of communion can recognize or ignore the assembly making this procession the prototype of McDonald's or the dim shape of the banquet to which we are invited.

All these rites of communion, from the Lord's Prayer to the silence before the concluding prayer, involve the most personal attention of each member of the assembly. We are ready to be at prayer in these moments, but on most occasions little is asked or expected of us. The ministry of the assembly— children, adults, all together—is quite clear. No great changes in any rites are needed, only the development of the assembly which lets us all do what our rites require of us.

Another sign of the cross, a word of farewell from the presider, perhaps a good song or some music, and our formal prayer together ends. It ends abruptly like many gatherings, but presumes the lingering time for business and visiting that follows.

That is what an assembly does. It may feel somewhat different with a hundred thousand people in a great outdoor liturgy than it does with a dozen people in a home, different with a bunch of ten-year olds than it does at a nursing home. But not very different, because assembly is a basic and human activity. The *Directory for Masses with Children* spoke of this humanity as what the assembly does at Mass.[4] This is merely the human foundation, but we are going nowhere without it.

"The activity of the community" should be experienced in the gathering, gestures, silence, sharing of bread and wine, and giving of thanks. "Expression of gratitude" should be experienced in the eucharistic prayer. "Experience of symbolic actions," like the gesture of the cross or the reaching out in the gesture of peace, should take on a dimension of care and beauty by which they express the otherwise inexpressible. "A meal of friendship" is a human experience which should be identified easily by the participants at the Sunday Mass. These actions clearly speak to the ministry of the assembly.

The Home: The Primary Assembly

The second area of importance in considering assembly is the home, the primary community. For some this may be one person, living alone or with others; for others, it is the family; and for others, it is the religious community.

Schools and other small groupings also enter into this. There is nowhere else we can learn to be assembly, learn about meals of friendship, festive celebrations, symbolic actions; exchanging greetings, listening, pardoning, seeking pardon, saying thanks.

Whatever prepares a child for the Eucharist takes place at home in the reality of the communion within the family's shared meals. *The Directory for Masses with Children* noted that it is ". . . not right to separate eucharistic formation for the general human and Christian education of children." If in our everyday lives we have come to think of eating as routine, of meals as chores, of supper together as rushed, and of food only as nourishment, then it will be difficult to communicate to our children the simple faith that Christians encounter Jesus in a meal.

If every other gesture of our lives makes the meal something cheap and uncomfortable, then we will not know the faith that brings people together on Sundays to bless and share bread and wine. We learn to be the assembly around all the tables. When we do not know the wonder of food and fellowship at home, then we cannot know what it is we come together on Sundays to do. We are a living contradiction if we try on Sundays to believe in the fellowship of the table, the awesome beauty of bread and wine, the good of human festivity, and yet live our daily lives without respect for food or fellowship of the table. We are able to find holiness in the bread that is blessed and shared in the assembly of Christians only if we find holiness in all the fruit of the earth by which we are nourished and brought together. Ours is a very earthy religion which is about the fullness of our lives. Our central gesture of prayer asks nothing more than bread, wine, and ourselves.

We learn to be assembly at home when taking meals together has priority for parents over other demands on their time. This should happen in an atmosphere of sharing, waiting, and the beauty of the table. Consider the tension between Eucharist-as-meal and Eucharist-as-sacrifice. "The tension calls one to remember that however elegant the knowledge of the dining room may be, it begins in the soil, in the barnyard, in the slaughter-house, amid the quiet violence of the garden, strangled cries, and fat spitting in the pan. Table manners depend on something's having been grabbed by the throat."[5]

The human capacity to delight in food and fellowship is so natural, yet it seems challenged in every time and culture. In our own times, a terrible line is drawn between those who have enough food and those who do not. There is the abundance of foods, even of good foods, and the lack of time to be at peace with them. It is really difficult to learn to bless God and enjoy the fruits of the earth, let alone to make a habit of it. It is very hard to create a home where this way of life gets lived.

In the blessing over the meal, we learn to be the assembly: to praise and thank God for the gift of God's presence in the gifts of the earth and in the gathered people. We learn to bless God when we gather at table. We need to create a sense of this blessing with the appropriate gesture and song. We make a home with the words, sounds, gestures, and objects of ordinary days, of Sundays, and of the seasons. We make the place where we belong.

The eucharistic action of our assembly keeps our worship from separating itself from our life. We cannot learn to do this well as a thing in itself, detached from our bodies, hunger, and human sharing. Lives that go on quite well six days a week without prayer will go on quite well without prayer on Sunday. Lives where the art of prayer, however simple, is not practiced will not know what prayer should be in the assembly. When there is prayer at home in the daily lives of people, they create their common prayer. Traditional church rituals in themselves cannot create a praying people; they can only strengthen and inspire. The formation of a life that needs prayer is the task of struggling to live our gospel tradition all the time. It is in the way we eat and how we are together that praise, thanks, and Eucharist begin to be the core of our lives. But it is also in the way we first look at morning, the way we see one another and God's creation, and the way we struggle with suffering and injustice. Like the psalmist, we are ever learning to get angry, question, and challenge.

Other human values present in the assembly's celebration of Mass are rooted in the home: cooperation, respect for others, hospitality, and forgiving and forgetting. One other value deserves our special attention: the capacity to listen.

The Liturgy of the Word is not a one-of-a-kind activity. The telling of stories is a fundamental way in which any group that shares a way of life communicates with itself. But storytelling and listening can't be that if they are left to Sundays alone. That ritual storytelling demands that storytelling and storylistening be familiar deeds. In the home, we learn to listen, to reflect, and to respond to stories. And eventually, we learn to tell stories.

Our problem is not a short supply of stories but the lack of the art of listening, and of listening together. As with our failure to surround meals with respect, there is a cheapening of the story. There is a tendency to treat stories as consumer products: something I buy, use, perhaps enjoy, and discard. We have little sense of a communal dimension, even when we sit in a full movie house or are one of twenty-million persons watching a television program. The problem is with our practice—parents and children seldom see or hear the same stories—and our attitude is one of consumption rather than sharing. We take in one after another without enjoyment or reflection.

As a Church, we expect the telling of our story to be crucial in a lifelong formation process. A part of the assembly's action, called liturgy, is storytelling. But there must be a respect for the story very much like our respect for food. In a culture that treats both as consumer products, we must learn to treat food and story as gifts of God, graces and bonds of the community. This comes not from some theology of story but with practice in homes where we strive to be listeners, to reflect and to respond in sharing.

Respect for stories and sharing begins with the good literature available for young children like fairy tales and some modern stories as well as scripture. Parents must be free to delight in these stories—the good ones cut across all age boundaries. They are the stories which Rosemary Haughton has said tell not so much what life is *like* as what *life* is like. As a child grows, the world of characters, lands, and situations expands in a common vocabulary with parents, brothers and sisters. The child comes to know what is a true story. The child and the adult go on to learn what Willa Cather said, "There are only two or three human stories. And they go on telling themselves as fiercely as if they had never happened before."

That is what we can learn about stories when we cease to consume them and start to share them. The attitude toward story that a tribe needs for the Liturgy of the Word to happen is that the story, because it is a *true* story, a well-crafted and well-told story, is *my* story. It happened to me; it happened to us. An assembly needs this sense of story to do the liturgy.

There is much we can do now to make Sunday eucharistic liturgy become the prayer of the assembly. We can develop our skills at story-telling and attune our consciousness of silence and prayer to the steady and strong ritual that liturgy should be for the length of a Christian's life. But there is much we can only begin to do now: we can only plant the seeds of good rituals, story-telling and a life of praise with our children. When we realize that our spiritual lives and our "real" lives are one life, and that the liturgical process starts in the home, then we will understand that the work of the everyday rituals and of the everyday itself is the foundation of the assembly.

NOTES

1. See "Ministries and Roles in the Celebration of Baptism," in *The Rite of Baptism with Children* (Washington, D.C.: United States Catholic Conference, 1969): "The people of God, that is the Church, made present in the local community, has an important part to play in the baptism of both children and adults."
2. See *Christian Initiation, General Introduction* (Washington, D.C.: United States Catholic Conference, 1969), 7: "In the actual celebration, the people of God should take an active part. Thus they will show their common faith and express their joy as the newly baptized are received into the community of the Church."
3. *Environment and Art in Catholic Worship* (Washington, D.C.: United States Catholic Conference, 1978), 7.
4. See *Directory for Masses with Children* (Washington, D.C.: United States Catholic Conference, 1973), 9: "In this way even if children already have some feeling for God and the things of God, they may also experience the human values which are found in the eucharistic celebration, depending upon their age and personal progress. These values are the activity of the community, exchange of greetings, capacity to listen and to seek and grant pardon, expression of gratitude, experience of symbolic actions, a meal of friendship, and festive celebration."
5. Aidan Kavanagh, *The Shape of Baptism* (New York: Pueblo Publishing, 1978), p. 160.

9

Seasons
Gabe Huck

My task is to examine the meaning of seasons for liturgical celebrations. To do this I need to examine one season in depth—Advent—and then to present some general considerations for seasons in liturgical planning.

Advent: The Season for Christmas[1]

Time is a good friend and a bitter enemy. Time is an important but elusive part of our lives. We can't say what it is nor can we get outside it to have a look. We become conscious of time when we have to wait, like during those everyday delays at the bus stop or subway station. We learn about time when we experience that inflexible law of nature at the service station or the bank: the other line always moves faster. And there are the bigger confrontations with time when we wait for justice, for an end to loneliness, or for death. Time and the waiting can slip beyond our control.

There is one very special waiting: the waiting for birth. In E. B. White's *Charlotte's Web*, after the good spider Charlotte has died, her friend Wilbur watches over the egg sac she left. "Patiently he awaited the end of winter and the coming of the little spiders. Life is always a rich and steady time when you are waiting for something to happen or to hatch."

Rich and steady, it depends. We wait for something to happen: the children to grow up, the mortgage to be paid, or a chance to make a difference in someone's life. Always, we wait for the hour of our death. Although not an easy time, there is a richness and steadiness in the waiting for these happenings.

While we wait—for growing up, old, or better time or peace—we have a time each year that takes us as Christians deeply into this part of being human. We call Advent those weeks of December that lead us to Christmas. The days grow shorter and shortest, until just before Christmas there comes a day when the sun is feebly but surely reborn.

Advent is our time for telling the stories about our waiting. "Joseph, son of David, have no fear about taking Mary as your wife. It is by the Holy Spirit that she has conceived this child. She is to have a son and you are to name him Jesus because he will save his people from their sins." It takes silence to hear these stories, a space within us where we let them touch our own longing and hope for fullness. Advent has its sounds and its colors that begin to reveal this space within us. There are words from the stories and songs of Advent that all by themselves make us feel that these days are telling a story about us, about me.

Advent represents a dark space for our waiting where we light candles and then gather to learn of the beauty of the dark and the light. The presence of the darkness tells us that we can't separate this waiting from our fear. We want this scary darkness to go away. We want things to be clear, bright, warm, and certain. We want and need the light.

In the cold parts of the world, people have held festivals on the shortest days of the year: a time to come together and to step out of the scary dark. Now we live in bright cities and towns sheltered from the dark and the cold. But the rites of Advent require us to light candles and to come together for warmth and light. Advent teaches us, "Do not be afraid!" We are still frightened of the dark and of much else, an economy we don't understand and what our children's futures will be.

At no other place or time do we feel this more than in December, when people snatch at real festivity to draw them together and shatter their quiet fears. But we find that nothing will build a festival when we search among the spiritless where there is no quiet to grasp steady time or to listen to promises. The promises of Advent are about not being afraid; but these are promises that can only be heard by those who have known fear. Our fears are not chased away like bad dreams when Christmas comes: we have made one another afraid and our lifetime work is to transform that fear into trust. Advent offers the room and the time for our private and shared fears to hear this promise. Advent is made out of ourselves and our communities; and so it mixes delight and anxieties, dread and gladness, as it speaks to and for the bully that is in all of us as well as the coward and the prophet. With all those ears we listen, with all those eyes we look, and with all those tongues we speak.

Throughout our scriptures, there are the stories of birth: Eve, Sarah, Rachel, Elizabeth, and Mary. So it happens with all living things: one generation conceives and gives birth to and raises another. This is our own story. Birth is what binds it all together and yet it is so special that we never cease to marvel when the child is born.

The Church announces the wintertime festival of a birth. Like other peoples, we chose the days when the sun turns around to have a birthday festival. The Romans had their winter birthday of the Unconquered Sun. People wait for this moment when the days stop growing shorter and there is the promise of a much longer day with time for growth and warmth. The promise of life in that returning sun sparks the festival of life's greatest moment. Birth in the normal course of things is an event of springtime when the newborn can thrive in the warmth and grow strong in summer and fall. But this birth is celebrated now out of time, when there should be no birth. This is a birth that turns around all that we had expected.

When it comes time to tell this story, it is saved for the darkness, the great womblike darkness of a winter night when the story can be told by bells, light, colors, and words we know well: "In those days Caesar Augustus published a decree ordering a census of the whole world . . . Everyone went to register . . . and so Joseph went from the town of Nazareth in Galilee to Judea to David's town of Bethlehem." And then Mary, the baby, the manger, angels, shepherds, glory, and peace.

Mary had a baby! The simple core of the story fills the first night of this festival. But when we gather to tell it at midnight with words and carols, it comes with other tales: "The people who walked in darkness have seen a great light. For the yoke that burdened them, the pole of their shoulder, and the rod of their taskmaster you have smashed." A smashed yoke, smashed task-master's rod, these are not happy images but they tell the part of the story which teaches the meaning of birth: an end of one thing so that something new can be set into motion. All this is gathered into the stories of Christmas, the martyred Stephen and the angry King Herod who dispatched his soldiers to slay all the very young boys of Bethlehem. One of T. S. Eliot's Magi says that though he had always thought birth and death were different, "This birth was hard and bitter agony for us, like Death, our death."

The mysterious is there in these stories. The best songs and poems of Christmas signify that this birth is no holiday of sentimentality, but stirs us to our depths for it is caught up in *my* birth and *my* death. Kenneth Patchen's poem says it best:

> The cold, swollen face of war leans in the window.
> They are blowing out the candles, Mary . . .
> The world is a thing gone mad tonight.
> O hold him tenderly, dear Mother,
> For His is a kingdom in the hearts of men.

This festival is no sweet anniversary of the day baby Jesus was born; nor is it humanity's bow to the noble ideal of peace on earth. This is a real festival: a time out of time. We give notice to the Herodlike world that its ways and days are numbered, for Mary had a baby and she called him Jesus: God fell in love with us, the Word was made flesh and dwelled among us.

This is at the heart of the Christmas festival. The things we do give spirit to the festival: gift-giving; exchanges of greetings; gatherings around beautiful tables; singing; and the keeping of the festival through the days until Epiphany. Through the following days the story unfolds and brings forward all sorts of images of saints and events until Epiphany when we mark what it means to be born. Then, all the senses know that Jesus is the Messiah when he is shown to the world, to the foreigners who follow the star, to the wedding guests at Cana who rejoice with wine made from water, and to those at the river Jordan when John baptizes him. The wonder of the darkness and the goodness of the light which highlighted our song and story through the waiting days of Advent and the festive days of Christmas come together on Epiphany to be the Lord's brightness shining on the holy city.

Through this festival, our task is to allow the story to overpower us. This is a "once upon a time" story which is truer than the temperature and time of day. Something in us thrills to hear of a birth and is absolutely convinced that things hold together because God is mixed up with our clay. When we are swept off our feet in this yearly retelling we know that the Christmas prayer which springs from this story isn't rooted in theological explanations but in all those human arts which touch the story and open up its myriad wonders.

Seasons: General Considerations
for Liturgical Planning

The meaning of Lent and Easter could be examined in a similar manner to Advent and Christmas. The general principles and directions of liturgical planning would be identical. All of this must be considered within the context of Sunday as the original feast day of Christians and the scriptural meaning of Sabbath-keeping. The following are central points in understanding and planning of liturgical seasons.

1. The cycle is a whole. The keeping of seasons is not one aspect of Church life that exists alongside doctrines, morality, and the sacraments. The seasons bring everything else into a common home. What we as Church have to learn is not taught in the classroom, but from the experience of and in a believing assembly. In this, the cycle of the year is the great teacher and the endless cause of study, meditation, and reconciliation.

The cycle is a whole. It is within the repetition of this cycle that the Church can create a sense of familiarity for the assembly. These patterns of shared experiences create a sense of belonging. This belonging builds gradually in the rituals when we can express in symbol what we mean and believe. It builds when this is a steady and repeated happening. Christian formation is deeply involved with the naming of days and the keeping of seasons as a way we grow up as this people. The matter of the rootedness of seasons in our parishes cannot be a matter for cute children's projects or superficial family customs that play around on the surface of real life.

2. *The cycle of our seasons is engaging for the whole person;* it covers every part of being human: from the fear of Advent to the disciplines of Lent. Yet it is a common occurence to find ourselves searching for a theme for a feast that we can fasten on to and use to plan the liturgy. This is our downfall. We think that the seasons are out there, an object to be sliced up and presented to our congregations. One of the problems is this outlook: that the season sits out there somewhere waiting for us to interpret it. The seasons are not out there, they are inside us. We need to let fear, hope, joy, anger, sorrow, compassion, desire, and delight come to life in the festivity of the assembly's ritual. These things cannot be expressed in prose, but in song, dance, and story.

The seasons are about living and dying. We have to stand back to let the realities of the words, colors, and sounds of the seasons echo within us. Seasons and festivals are dimensions of the scripture tradition which identify our faith community. The ways we keep the seasons evolve in the hands of those who know that the seasons are as vital to us as they were to our ancestors. There are no new fears or dreams, only new occasions for them. The ritual of the season is strong when it draws out that fear or dream in the present just as it did in the past.

3. *The cycle of the seasons is commonplace.* It is not the special realm of scholars, mystics, or any one class within the Church. The seasons are of the people. This is where the naming of days and seasons has always happened. We do not set out to invent or re-invent the seasons. The liturgies of the seasons must know the primacy of the assembly. The prayer of the seasons must have the words and gestures that can bring meaning to individuals and families everyday. This prayer has everything to do with respect for ourselves and for ritual as the full human expression of what matters in our lives.

4. *The cycle of the seasons is inexhaustible.* The stories we tell through our seasons are so simple that they can never fully be known no matter how many times we live through the cycle. It is our own story we are telling and we will never know it fully. We see this more clearly each year: no two Christmases are the same; no hundred Christmases exhaust what Christmas means. Only the power of repetition brings this sense of appreciation. If we try to celebrate Advent one way this year and completely differently the next, we get nowhere because we are the ones who change. The very beauty of this dimension of liturgy cannot take root unless we respect the importance of yearly repetition.

5. *The cycle of the seasons has a rhythm.* There are the long times and the short times, the greater festivals and the lesser festivals. More importantly, there is the rhythm of anticipation, celebration, and continuation. Within

that rhythm is our home, our sense of belonging, and our recognition of the sensed things about a festival. This rhythm gives the seasons their presence and familiarity which allows them to transform the Church from generation to generation and ties us to the larger rhythm of *my* life. The Church offers hospitality to those who approach, cares for them and is challenged by them, as it unfolds its life within the repeated flow of the seasons.

    6. At present, the cycle of the seasons is counter-cultural. It is not a part of being an American these days to give priority to holy days or festivals that in their essence have no practical purpose. This is no passing conflict of culture and those who would keep seasons and festivals as Church. This is an area which demands our attention and reminds us that the seeds for the Christian life are sown and nurtured in the home.

    Josef Pieper expresses the meaning of the seasons when he writes, "Inability to be festive, on the other hand, can be explained in such a way as to illuminate the core of the problem. It signifies 'immurement' within the zone of the given present, 'exposure to the terrors of history.' Festivity, on the other hand, is a liberation. Through it the celebrant becomes aware of, and may enter, the greater reality which gives a wider perspective on the world of everyday work, even as it supports it."[2]

    The naming and the keeping of days breaks down the world's walls. Walls which can become very comfortable for some of us. Walls which separate the parts inside each of us, and which separate us from the others who should be as one with us at prayer.

NOTES

    1. The first part of this presentation is based on my *Naming the Days*, a set of filmstrips and cassettes published by *Our Sunday Visitor*.

    2. Josef Pieper, *In Tune With the World: A Theory of Festivity*, trans. Richard and Clara Winston (Chicago: Franciscan Herald Press, 1973), p. 32.

10

Drama, Liturgy, and Children
Thomas A. Kane

For the International Conference on Liturgy for Young Christians I was asked to lead a workshop on drama, children, and liturgy for an adult audience. Planning the presentation was a challenge since there would be no children present, and talking about drama seemed to defeat the very nature of the art form. I decided to involve the whole group in a participation event.

Everyone would be invited to enter into the doing of drama. We would all be participants. There would be no spectators or outsiders looking in. I felt that the group needed to experience the dramatic forms directly, thus illustrating and reinforcing the power of *being* the story and *living* the drama of the scriptures.

The workshop was organized into four parts: the *Presentation*—to introduce the relationship of liturgy to the dramatic elements of ritual, experience, and celebration; the *Film*—to provide an example of the effective use of drama in proclaiming a scripture story; the *Planning*—to engage the participants in the making of a drama; and the *Performing*—to involve each person directly in the dramatic presentation. In describing this workshop in print, I have expanded and reworked the material to involve the reader as much as possible.

At the start of the session, I discussed the limitations of talking about drama and shared how I worked with children in liturgical drama. From my own work, I extracted three significant areas of interaction of liturgy with drama.

Liturgy as Ritual
The word "ritual" evokes different images. For some, it is a negative term implying rigidity, tradition—something done out of habit, force, or custom. It limits freedom and can turn people into robots. For others, ritual is neutral and provides ways to cope with everyday life. Still others see ritual as a distinctly positive way of ordering reality. Ritual can structure a celebration for a group or community gathering, be it political, social, or religious.

For Christians, ritual is the dramatic language of religion which gives shape and form to what we believe and hold dear. Ritual *speaks*. It uses every mode of human communication. Words, images, sounds, shapes, and movements join together in creating the whole. Ritual *impacts*. As a polysensual experience, it touches the total person and draws all the senses into active participation.

Liturgical renewal needs to be constantly reminded of the ritual dimension of worship because this is the meeting place of the human spirit. Religious ritual allows men and women to keep in tune with the natural world by exploring the hidden meaning of life. Through festivity, we can transform the ordinary into the special. Through celebration we can get in touch with our deepest human struggles and recognize the spark of the divine.

The dramatic forms of ritual help us experience a story by living it, encounter a mystery by entering it, and meeting a person by remembering him. By being a part of the telling, the perspectives shift and those involved have a stake in what is happening. The senses become more alert, emotional energy is released, and the person becomes alive to the eternal moment.

This vitality is shared by all participants in the ritual as the body channels spirit, mystery, and new life. Religious ritual, then, is not abstract conjuring, but the encounter of the whole person with ultimate reality. The present recalls the past and projects a future.

Liturgy as Experience

The root definition of liturgy is "work of the people"—something people do. The very meaning of the word includes the sense of participation and involvement. So often we hear that our Sunday worship is to come out of our experience of faith in God. On Sunday we gather to give thanks and praise to God for the gift of Jesus. By celebrating God's mighty deeds in Jesus, we connect our local community to the larger community of Christians. The aim of our Sunday worship is to touch the deep chords within our daily experience and to challenge and inspire us.

For many Christians, Sunday is a day of gloom, boredom, and abstract ritualizing. In the past, liturgy was often confined to a written text contained within the pages of the book; it was something that required absolute conformity. This rubrical approach often prevented worship from becoming the prayer of an alive community and stifled any possibilities for creative expression.

Children can often help teach adults to rediscover and trust their experience. In many schools of religion, children are encouraged to bring their full selves into worship and to make worship part of their entire life. Sensitive television programming and contemporary religious texts stress the reflective experience, speaking to children where they live.

In teaching the Eucharist to second graders, for example, emphasis is placed on the family meal or the birthday party. Through the experience of eating and partying together, the child sits with the family of God at table celebrating the memory of Jesus by singing, dancing, and being quiet—expressing thanks in so many different ways. The meaning is not imposed or memorized but comes from the experience of sharing the Bible stories (word) and the meal (sacrament).

The experience of children today may be very rich and unique yet differ from the adult viewpoint. One year when I taught a First Communion class, I was amazed at how quickly the children were able to relate their own experiences of party and meal to Eucharist. They had no problem in talking about Jesus' presence, and class presentations went smoothly until we rehearsed the actual liturgy. At Communion time, there were snickers and giggles. After some questioning, I was able to discover that the wafer-hosts were the source of the commotion. The children had never seen hosts closeup and were very curious about them. They were able to accept the host as special to church, but could not make the connection with bread. They told me right out that bread was fluffier, had more texture and didn't crack when broken. As it turned out, the act of faith for these second graders was not that Jesus was present in the bread and wine, but that the small wafer was actually bread.

Liturgy as Celebration

Celebration is a defiant act. It is deeply rooted in the very texture of our being and calls forth from each of us—words, song, and dances—joyful, soulful, and sometimes sad. To celebrate is to express our connection with God, the world and people around us. Celebration is a wonderful word to use in conjunction with worship because it opens up so many possibilities for people of all ages.

One of these possibilities is dramatizing the Word of God. The scriptures are so rich in stories, events, and characters which lend themselves to a dramatic presentation. To dramatize the scriptures is to embody them, to make them part of the texture of our very being. When used in a liturgical setting, scriptural drama can be a powerful event for all involved.

The dramatic element of worship is built into every service with the colors of the seasons, the stories of faith, and the very settings of our church buildings. The dramatic is part of *how* we worship, drawing us into the mystery of God's saving activity.

Sometimes, as adults, we can lose our childlike sense of openness and trust. We forget to look and are afraid to feel. Within the liturgy, dramatic forms can unleash the creative potential, help us see the gospel message with fresh eyes and receive the good news with fleshy hearts. Drama can touch us as well as enhance the overall liturgy.

With children or adults for that matter, there are two basic ways to use the scripture texts directly. The first involves giving each person a character from the story and acting out the passage in the sanctuary or throughout the Church during the Liturgy of the Word. Another approach, which I personally favor in working with young people under twelve years of age, is to rehearse two or more readers separately and use them as the voices of the reading and have the other children mime or roleplay the action.

Last year I worked with about fifteen children from the ages of four to thirteen. Some of the young people were handicapped and in wheelchairs. After meeting with the group and discussing different scripture stories, we selected the story of Noah's Ark because enacting it could involve everyone.

In rehearsal, I met with smaller groups of children and talked about the meaning of the story, and I asked them to select a favorite animal and to think about how that animal would move and sound. In a short time there was a veritable menagerie taking shape.

I played the narrator of the story and one of the older boys played Noah. As I began the story of the Ark, Noah began creating the shape of an Ark on the floor with logs. It was a large Ark to hold all the children, especially those in wheelchairs.

After the Ark was completed, I mentioned the various animals Noah selected for his Ark. At this point each child came forward when his animal was mentioned. Some wore colored shirts to suggest their animal, others created the effect with sound and gesture. There were hopping kangaroos, hissing snakes, delicate butterflies, barking dogs, and cuddly cats. The children in the wheelchairs gestured with their arms to accompany their imaginative animal sounds.

Once the Ark was filled, two children imitated the sound of rain, and one carried a bolt of lightning to suggest the storm. The storm was practically a dance around the Ark. The animals cowered down to the ground until the rain passed. After sending forth the dove, which circled the Ark and brought back a green leaf, Noah smiled as a rainbow was uncovered on the back wall. The drama ended with everyone singing a familiar Noah song about God's love and the rainbow.

The experience was a good one because everyone could select a specific character, develop it imaginatively, and contribute to the entire effort. The children in the wheelchairs were especially thrilled to be able to play a part from the scriptures. The drama brought everyone close together physically and spiritually.

Using drama with young people can tap into the wellspring of their experience. Children enjoy taking on different characters, writing their own plays, putting on costumes, or being part of a scripture story. The dramatic context is one way to help children connect the Christian story with their own life story. By enacting the scriptures within the liturgy, the children and all of us can begin experiencing worship as vital and nourishing to our growth as Christians.

The Group Process

After this presentation, we screened Marcel Marceau's *Creation of the World,* which portrayed a mime version of the Genesis story. My purpose was to illustrate another way of presenting the scriptures and to awaken the creative juices of the conference participants.

After the film, the larger group was broken down into smaller working groups. Each group received a copy of the creation narrative from Genesis and was asked to design a dramatic version of the story with or without words. The groups had about seventy-five minutes to design, rehearse, and stage their work.

When the conference reassembled, each group presented their dramatic interpretation of creation. The presentations were stunning. Each group devised a different story structure for their material. One group chose an "organic approach" where everyone huddled together as raw matter, with faces hidden. As the narrator told the story, the group would undulate and give birth to the variety of creation. The different creatures would rise up from the middle of the group with radiant faces. Thus, from chaos God produced a beautiful world teeming with animals, fish, and soaring birds.

Another group used music as the unifying motif. Standing in a large circle, they combined the narrative text with a liturgical song. During each refrain, the group would shape different aspects of creation. By the end of the song, the circle was filled with all types of creatures. The third group used a storyteller while the rest of the group mimed the creative elements and characters. There were jackrabbits, butterflies, rhinoceroses, and songbirds with Adam and Eve in the center of Eden.

Throughout the presentations, there was laughter, tears, prayer, and a great outpouring of creativity. The group process brought the conference participants closer together, and by the end of the workshop, there was a sense of solidarity, awe, and wonder at how much creativity was contained in the groups and at how much fun it all was. The drama-sharing aided in community building, in reinforcing friendships, and in underscoring the power of the creative process. By entering into the dramatic process, the participants became aware of the lived reality of ritual celebration. In a very real way, there was a feeling of transformation and renewal combined with a new awareness of sharing in God's creation.

Postscript

The power of drama was driven home to me a few years after this conference when I was in France for a meeting with liturgists. After dinner one evening, a rather serious-looking German scholar approached me. As he came nearer, he began to smile. I was quite certain he had mistaken me for someone else.

"Don't you recognize me?" he asked. I looked at him, but couldn't place him. "I was in Washington for the conference," he replied. I hadn't the foggiest who this man was or what conference he attended.

To relieve my anxiety, I politely asked, "Did you enjoy the conference?"

"Yes," he responded, "but you forget." I was still confused.

"Thomas," he said, "Nancy and I were butterflies."

"Oh," I said haltingly, "you were a butterfly."

An image flashed into my mind, and suddenly there was clarity. This man had been at the International Conference and had taken part in the drama workshop. Of course, I remembered him. He was an exuberant butterfly.

"I still remember that day," he said. "Imagine, *me* a butterfly!"

We both laughed, hugged each other, and shared our story with the other liturgists.

The experience of being part of the creative process is something one doesn't easily forget. The drama was still a part of our bodies and our storytelling, a delightful memory of a prayerful moment when we rediscovered our own creative impulses by celebrating in a dramatic way what wonderful things God has done for us.

11

Liturgy for Young People:
The Present Situation in England
Edward Matthews

The time after Vatican II through the early 1970s was the time of the loose-leaf liturgy. Good celebration amounted to the more or less effective control of large quantities of paper scattered around the altar and lectern, like city streets the morning after a football game. Nowhere was this more true than in children's liturgies: required copies of the newly reformed texts were not yet included in any definitive version of the missal. Instead, there was a multiplicity of unofficial texts, adapted readings, prayers, and, most of all, eucharistic prayers.

In England, pieces of paper were about as far as we could go. Many other European countries were, with episcopal approval, publishing both directives and texts for the celebration of young people's liturgy. The official English attitude ranged from curious tolerance of simplified scripture readings to outright disapproval of anything which in any way deviated from the standard adult celebration. The most common approach was: "Only when Rome takes the initiative will we approve."

Rome did take the initiative. *Directory for Masses with Children*, followed soon after by the *Eucharistic Prayers with Children*, answered the needs and demands of many in England. The *Directory* gave official foundation for what appeared so necessary, and the new *Eucharistic Prayers* provided a certain sense of security in an area where indifferent and harmful materials had been circulating. What then is the situation in England today?

In many of our English-Catholic schools, parishes, and youth groups, there is a fresh, creative approach to liturgical celebration which is leading the young participants both to a deeper understanding of the mysteries they celebrate and to a firmer commitment to the Christian way of life. But I must confess that such successes are only in the minority. Having the opportunity to speak to groups of teachers and priests, I put to them the question, "How many of you have heard of the *Directory*?" Of teachers, about half answer affirmatively; of priests, less than half. "How many have used the *Eucharistic Prayers*?" Even fewer reply in the affirmative; and here the teacher is totally dependent on the priest. It could be argued that knowledge of official documents is no guide to the state of celebration, but on the English-Catholic scene that is not so. Despite the leadership of a few, a fully participatory liturgy for the young has hardly gotten off the ground.

English-Catholic parishes, like those throughout the world, come in all shapes and sizes, and on many levels of progress. Some are outstanding in their celebration; a few are abysmal; and many are shades in between. However, all too often one hears the teenager cry, "It's boring. I get nothing out of it," or as a girl once summed it up, "plastic prayer said by a plastic priest." Behind this lies the dominance of obligation over celebration. I look forward to the day when members of the community will be present because they wish to celebrate the saving events of our Redemption.

But are we celebrating events any more? Wherever I go we seem to be celebrating ideas. And this applies equally to children's liturgies as to adult liturgies. That fact is that our liturgy is becoming over-intellectualized; and the more it is intellectualized, so much the more does it become a liturgy of words. There is a distinct danger that our celebration will be thrown out of balance and that it will die under the sheer weight of verbiage. Perhaps this is one reason why so many of our young people find the liturgy boring. Our liturgical celebrations fail to take into account the many different ways in which we communicate with God, and God with us: we fail to take into account the whole human person.

A few parishes have introduced Sunday celebrations for children. These include a special Liturgy of the Word running alongside the adult celebration. These are invariably a great success, but we must resist the temptation to so concentrate on the needs of children that they finish up separated and remote from the main worshipping community. It is the parochial community, made of worshipping families, which is the heart of the local Church.

One of the most important challenges to the English-Catholic church is to establish a firm and lasting link between the worshipping community and family life. At the church's liturgy, we pray together; but at home, do we pray at all? The contrast between home and church practice may be so great as to lead to the rejection of this latter. We are desperately in need of the restoration of family prayer. It has died, but there are signs of resurrection. The charismatic movement and other prayer groups are already having a measurable effect upon the lives of some families and hence upon the liturgy. The growth of prayer may well lead to the growth of celebration.

The reasons for this state of affairs are diverse, but they are reasons which apply not only to young people's liturgy but to the entire English-Catholic scene. First, there is the problem of the English character, which generally speaking is one of reserve and a fear of demonstrativeness. The Sign of Peace has been branded "un-English." If that is a problem with adult liturgy, you can well imagine the personal difficulties of adults assisting at the celebrations of young people where so much more is demanded by way of openness and demonstrativeness. And we must consider the English dislike of change and their deep love of tradition, frequently tradition for tradition's sake. The freedom and adaptation demanded by the liturgical celebration of young people poses a serious question to those, who by birth and upbringing, regard with unmitigated suspicion any practice which has not been in existence for at least four hundred years!

Second, the slow liturgical development in England can be traced to another aspect of tradition. From 1553 until 1778, with only one brief interruption, Roman Catholics in England were systematically persecuted. The celebration of Mass was forbidden; to be a priest was treason. Hundreds of English-Catholics were executed, often in a most barbaric manner, and the estates of most English-Catholic landowners were confiscated. The English-Catholic community was embattled and continually on the defensive. Although emanicipation from almost all civil disabilities came about in 1829, the history of that difficult period still colors English-Catholic attitudes today.

Any alteration in the celebration of Mass is regarded by some as a "sell-out" to Protestantism, a denial of all that the English-Catholic martyrs signify. Therefore, adaptation to the needs of young people is seen as a weakness which is unworthy of the memory of our courageous forebears. The English Reformation turned upon the question of obedience to Rome. English-Catholics lived and died for it; and today a slavish attitude is often adopted to the edicts emanating from the *Curia*. To be more precise, there is an inability in many to make mature use of legitimate freedom. Instead, they maintain a never-ending desire for decisions, rulings, and definitions from central authority. While this attitude is not shared by all English-Catholics, it is certainly present in the majority of the English-Catholic leaders. The *Directory for Masses with Children* is a problem because it advocates a flexibility in approach to celebration. It does not satisfy the needs of some for exact and minute guidance in all aspects of that celebration. To become master of one's own liturgy seems like a denial of English-Catholic history.

Third, the slow progress of children's liturgy is due to the lack of liturgical education—a problem not unique to England, but one shared with many other countries, particularly the English-speaking ones. The *Directory* is a straightforward application of liturgical principles governing participation and adaptation. If those principles are not understood, one of two things happens: either the liturgy is wrecked by an overeager desire to chop and change at all costs, or little to no change takes place.

I do not want to paint a completely bleak picture. The majority of teachers and priests have made great efforts to come to grips with the challenges presented by the renewed liturgy. The unfortunate situation is that the means of liturgical changes have been communicated to those working at the pastoral level as if the entire matter were simply a case of substituting new rubrics for old. This lack of liturgical understanding afflicts not only celebrations for young people but those for adults as well. Priests who are good celebrants for children are nearly always good celebrants for adults, a rule that holds good in the reverse direction also.

12

Planning Our Sacred Play
G. Thomas Ryan

The words in this or any other resource book remain vague ideals or fuel for frustration unless translated onto the local scene. In books about the sacred play of children, the arena for implementation is most obviously the local church. While these holy buildings are the primary sites for Christian common prayer, they are not the only places. Our homes, apartments, convalescence centers, hospitals, cemeteries, parks, and dining halls can be places for prayer. Wherever we Christians gather for worship, we are the Church incarnate there. The heritage of eucharistic Christians maintains that this is most true at the table of the Lord. For there the Church is formed and sustained. Thus it is at those assemblies that this book's ideals should be most evident.

When prayer forms seem moribund—and especially when the eucharist seems distant or "irrelevant"—Christians have every reason to be upset. As adults and children, we want our common treasure to ennoble us, to form us as the Body of Christ. It is no secret that many members of the Church, perhaps many purchasers of this book, experience this frustration, even anger. The questions "When will the Church pay attention to its children?" and "What can we do to improve this?" are heard in every region. The latter question is less an offer to help the parish than a cry of frustration—what can we, the laity, do when the liturgy is so complex and when the clergy are in command?

This article will look at some of the ways to implement the goals of prayerful children's liturgies, especially eucharistic liturgies. It will focus on the action which takes place before we even gather around the table. Rather than providing helpful hints for each part of the worship service, this piece will look at planning. At this level we might find some relief for prevailing frustrations.

Every local church has some form of worship planning. Even if it is only the pastor consulting with the sexton or the organist selecting four hymns, there is advance work. If our liturgies are to be truly prayerful and inviting for all ages, then this work is best shared by many in the congregation. This increased involvement will need coordination and careful implementation or the planning participation will be ineffectual and short-lived.

There are, of course, churches where the pastors refuse to see the obvious need for planning. While they might see their own work as liturgy planning, they are confused or even ignorant of the laity's role. Bishops, synods, and liturgy experts fill clergy conferences and newsletters with background material and practical ideas, but progress is slow. Perhaps the resistance to planning participation stems from a jealous guarding of the clerical prerogative, or, more positively stated, a fear that the laity will not understand the correct flow of the established worship order.

As the Roman Catholic Church was reviewing its entire liturgical repertoire during the 1960s and early '70s, the Vatican Congregations and Committees began to reiterate (or, in some cases, state for the first time) that the whole assembly should have a hand in the preparation for liturgy. The 1969 Vatican document outlining the reformed rites for eucharistic celebration is called the *General Instruction of the Roman Missal*. It lays out the basic need for congregational planning:

> The pastoral effectiveness of a celebration depends in great measure on choosing readings, prayers, and songs which correspond to the needs, spiritual preparation, and attitude of the participants. . . . In planning the celebration, the priest should consider the spiritual good of the assembly rather than his own desires. The choice of texts is to be made in consultation with the ministers and others who have a function in the celebration, including the faithful, for the parts which belong to them. Since a variety of options is provided, it is necessary for the deacon, readers, cantors, commentator, and choir to know beforehand the texts for which they are responsible, so that nothing shall mar the celebration. Careful planning and execution will help dispose the people to take their part in the eucharist. (#313)

This cordial consultation can be confusing and time-consuming, but it begins to reverse the all-too-prevalent frustrations in liturgy. First and foremost, the cooperation of the whole local church helps us all recognize that we make the Church, that we accept the gift of faith and membership in this common assembly. We do not rely on formal ritual books to make our prayer for us. We make our prayer and use the books (and bells and robes and water and so much else) to facilitate this action.

Planning Structures

Whether planning liturgies for children or for the whole congregation, we need to know both the people to be present and the ritual form to be used.

In terms of children's liturgies, are we planning "Masses with adults in which children also participate" or "Masses with children in which only a few adults participate"? These are the headings for two chapters in the official Roman Catholic *Directory for Masses with Children (DMC)*. They convey just one of the decisions to be made as planning begins. In this and in other areas of discernment we plan liturgies best by knowing our specific assembly.

This pushes concern for liturgy planning back to the broader context of pastoral ministry. Indeed, worship preparation is but one essential element in parish life. Good celebrations need a community, and each community needs good celebrations. The health of liturgy planning is usually one symptom of overall communal wholeness. Pastors and church members who know their local community, who readily and consistently minister to their peers, have the primary "skill" for planning common prayer.

Liturgy planning seen as part of pastoral ministry also means that all ministers should cooperate in worship preparation. When one member of a church staff ignores the priority of worship, or when any committee (budget, education, social justice, etc.) belittles its importance, the results become evident. Finances may be there for institution maintenance but not for liturgical participation aids. The associate pastor might have time for youth ski-trip planning, but not for homily preparation.

As in other facets of ministry, equal time will not—and perhaps should not—be spent by all. We are a community of diverse gifts. What is called for is an attitude which allows worship its primal role. There will also be certain decisions about prayer that need the input and perhaps agreement of all. For example, the annual (or monthly) calendars of each church should be planned by all in cordial consultation.

The specific tasks of liturgy planning will be facilitated if there is a sane and balanced schedule of events. Religious education classes, liturgy planning sessions, parish leadership meetings, and Bible study groups should not be all on the same evening. Parish festivals should not compete with the local high school graduation. Good Friday services should be scheduled so that most people can participate. Parish bingo must never compete with the Easter Vigil (indeed this has happened more than once!). Homilists and other liturgy leaders will also do their work better if other parish events leave liturgy and its planning the proper breathing space and time.

Besides the general planning of schedules, keeping liturgy as a priority, many congregations and pastors establish a specific liturgy committee. These groups go under many names: liturgy commission, worship planning, spiritual development commission, ritual committee, etc. There are almost as many variants as there are denominations or dioceses. While the titles multiply, the understandings of their purpose and their agenda are even more diverse. Nine of these numerous goals are identified here. Under each one we might find some elements of what we each want to do in our own settings.

These understandings of "liturgy committee" can help us all sift through the varied demands in planning. They might also help parish leaders review their structures so that more people can participate. In addition, this series of nine provides a checklist for children's worship planners.

Policy Making

Someone in every parish makes policy decisions about worship. It might be the pastor alone, or the organist, or the sexton. Perhaps it's the parish council or vestry or deacons. Maybe it's the liturgy committee that meets monthly or the pastor and secretary who meet daily. To help our parishes plan better liturgies, it will be useful to consider the decision-makers. Who sets the worship artifacts budget? Who interviews and decides on new musicians? Who allocates appropriate resources for big and small celebrations?

The people who do this should be the most involved Christians, and they must have a liturgical sense. Most importantly, they should be aware that they are setting policy (rather than stumbling into decisions) and that this work is a real ministerial service to their brothers and sisters.

Strategy Group

Sometimes liturgy preparation requires a great deal of attention to one issue. The community may need a new building for its worship, or some members might be calling for renovations to the existing space. A group of parents may step forward and demand more activities and liturgies for children. The musicians may call for a new hymnal. These needs have varying levels of complexity, but they all require more than one evening's debate.

Whether it's the ten-year project to build a new building or the six-month process to select and introduce new pew books, a full parish strategy must be planned and implemented. Depending on the project, a liturgy committee which becomes a "de facto" strategy team should invite the proper participants: architects, finance experts, musicians, audio specialists, teachers of young children, etc. Thus the personnel for this type of liturgy planning might be more specialized than the general worship policy makers. Again depending on the issue, the timing of meetings and setting of agenda will vary—often not fitting the monthly format.

Planning the Year

Since liturgical planning should be an integral part of overall parish planning, once a year some parish leaders should chart out a calendar that lets the key liturgical seasons and events stand out as important gatherings. Indeed, the fund raisers must plan to suspend the Saturday bingo on Easter eve. And, more broadly, the religious educators could set a curriculum that lets Sunday school or weekday classes mark and explain the liturgical seasons celebrated by adults and children. Without this kind of collaboration, Sunday worship must bear the weight not only of that worship, but also of explaining what that worship is all about.

The people involved in this calendar planning process are normally the representatives of the parish groups and programs which schedule activities. For the discussion to be realistic and the decisions to stand firm, these representatives will need an earlier meeting with their committee or guild, charting their specific needs and goals for the coming year. When all the forces within a local church gather to negotiate the optimum calendar, tensions or confusion may arise. Yet this in itself can help the process by suggesting a real evaluation of parish priorities. It also helps the church staff. Every priest or religious educator knows what it is like to have someone else plan on their presence at an event and then not tell them until the last minute when double-booking is probable.

Within the specific ministry of facilitating children's common prayer, this planning can assure an orderly flow of catechesis and celebration, of integration with the adult community, and of appropriate events for each age level during the year. For example, Catholic parishes may want a common Reconciliation service prior to Confirmation. Prior planning will recognize this need early enough to keep an evening free of other parish events. Thus families and other parish members might be able to join in the service.

Many churches which are attempting to serve their young members' needs use such a calendar discussion to establish a pattern of monthly children's or family liturgies. While there is some virtue in the ease of this pattern, it can do injustice to the liturgical year. Our Church calendar is Advent—Christmas and Lent–Easter, with the thirty-three other Sundays forming our regular rhythm. Our calendar is not January, February, etc. Holding these special liturgies on the third Sunday every month may mean they miss the whole Christmas season, observe Advent only at the end, etc. If twelve children's liturgies are what a parish wants, it is probably more appropriate to schedule them at the times when youth needs and liturgical calendar dictate. One example might be: All Saints (celebrated Halloween late afternoon), the First Sunday of Advent, Christmas, Valentine's Day, Ash Wednesday, Holy Week (a special session for catechesis and prayer on Wednesday, Thursday, or Friday to prepare them for full participation in the Easter Vigil), First Eucharist, Confirmation, Pentecost, the parish's anniversary or patronal day, and school's opening and closing.

Planning the Season

This form of planning may not necessitate as broad a representation. The work of establishing an annual schedule now gives way to more detailed plans for the liturgies of each season. The personnel for this effort can include some of those with the strongest personal investment. If youth are confirmed during the Easter season, some of the confirmands and/or their leaders could have a hand in shaping the season. Newly baptized adults from one year might help plan the next Lent–Easter cycle. Leaders of a summer vacation program may want input into plans for summer Sundays.

While participants may come with varied interests or constituencies, seasonal planning best begins with common reflection on the meaning and liturgical intent of that season. Then the group can chart the parish's observance: Sunday celebration ideas (decor, music), home prayer and activity suggestions which flow from the Sunday scriptures and worship, ways for the education and other programs to enhance and be enhanced by this season.

Planning the Worship Pattern

Whether written down or not, local churches have a standard pattern to their Sunday celebrations. Most accept and implement the standard rites for their tradition—Roman Catholics begin with the *Sacramentary* and *Lectionary* of the *Roman Missal*, Lutherans find common ground in the *Lutheran Book of Worship*, and Episcopalians share *The Book of Common Prayer*. Beyond these and similar volumes, all churches develop a local tradition. The psalm is always recited at the 7:30 A.M. service, sung by a cantor at the 9:00 A.M., and led by the choir at the 11:00 A.M. The acolytes always bow a certain way, or the lay readers have all been asked to pause for ten seconds between the reading introduction and text. Local customs also evolve for decorations, vesture, ushering, and lighting. The military has a code for this—SOP. Whenever a parish varies part of its Standard (or Standing) Operating Procedure, the congregation can tell.

The gradual upgrading of worship's quality begins with conscious knowledge of the SOP. When we know what is a particular service's normal opening rite, we can evaluate possible adaptations. We can formulate a new SOP, even if we don't write it down as such.

Some active Christians may be quite wary of such SOPs. How can prayer be from the heart if it is so predictable? When posed, this question often evidences a misunderstanding of ritual itself. Rites always involve SOP. They are repetition. Thus we can enter into common prayer without worrying about what will come next. When a prayer ends "through Christ our Lord," we know that "Amen" is our response. If we had to stop and think of the proper line each time, or if we had to follow a printed program alternating "Amen" with "So be it," "So it is," "May it be so," "Alleluia," and "Yes," the liturgy would become too intellectual, too verbal. The presence of a SOP should not mean liturgy by rote. It only becomes this if the SOP is too rigid, if the congregation lacks faith, or if some church leader stifles prayerful entrance into participatory ritual.

The identification of the standard pattern allows the liturgy committee to work at pieces of the pattern each year. One year the placement of music within the service flow might be improved. The next year the role of children might be studied and new practices to recognize them added to the SOP. This process will come as some relief to busy liturgy committees who have read that every liturgy must be carefully planned. Indeed, that is true, but the planning may be embellishing the SOP, not reinventing the wheel or the Eucharist.

Those with a keen interest in children's liturgies will find in chapters two and three of DMC a mine of practical ideas. They are intended as modifications for the SOP, not just one-time novelties.

Planning Specific Liturgies: Ongoing Committee

When it is time to turn from the overall planning listed above, most churches have an identifiable group which formulates each specific liturgy's order. Often the elements are decided by separate ministers—music director, homilist, presider, sacristan—and pieced together only during the event. Sometimes the procedure is more organized, with a representative group of congregation members collaborating with the ministers. When this group is formalized into an ongoing liturgy committee, the members can learn through continual planning. Leaders can enable new and veteran members to grow in liturgical knowledge. Those who help shape the common prayer can become comfortable with one another: planning, praying, learning, and even playing together.

When a church begins a series of children's liturgies, such a standing committee allows its planners to benefit from sharing and growth. Yet there are places where this sustained, year-round effort will limit participation by an already overwhelmed core of church volunteers. Thus there is another way to recruit and to empower liturgy planners.

Planning Specific Liturgies: Ad Hoc Committees

The difference between this and the ongoing liturgical committee is that the members gather only to plan one liturgy, then they disband. Some youth, parents, and catechists might join with the pastor and folk music leader to plan a junior high school liturgy. Meanwhile, parents of younger children, a mimer or storyteller, a kindergarten teacher, the youth choir leader, and associate pastor are planning a Halloween liturgy for young children. Some of these same people will meet later in the year with still others to plan Ash Wednesday, or Good Friday, or a summer picnic liturgy.

While the number of people involved can grow and their commitment is more focused, there is less opportunity for ongoing education. This deficiency can be addressed by encouraging a core of people to join such ad hoc groups with some frequency. Thus those becoming more adept at liturgical adaptation jump into active planning in those months when schedules permit. This also allows those most interested in particular holidays to plan those days. When someone leaves the Christmas family liturgy extolling its beauty, suggest right then that they help plan next year's!

Preparing Things

Liturgy is always incarnate. We who pray are not angels. We are sensate persons for whom the elements of this earth form an environment of prayer. Thus we use bread, wine, water, candles, vesture, palms, crosses, books, poetry, music, oil, and so much else. The preparation of these items is just as central to liturgy planning as is writing a homily. This aspect of preparation can involve whole new groups of people beyond the committee-types. Visual artists, potters, and firefighters may value common prayer yet have little taste for planning meetings. Their skills can still be part of the church's preparation when they paint wall-hangings, provide cups and flagons, and build a safe but visible Easter Vigil fire.

Within this phase of year-round worship work, those who try to adapt their sanctuaries for children's gatherings can be quite frustrated. The furnishings may be the wrong size for shorter participants or the unrenovated old building may inhibit fuller gestures, movement, or dance. This is a good opportunity to learn that the liturgy planning meeting does not just dictate the artifacts and space to be used. The process operates just as much in the reverse. The space and available materials invite the liturgy to take certain shapes and not others. Planners may begin by calling for a Palm Sunday procession of all—from school to church or up and down all the aisles. But if the neighborhood and the building itself do not allow any such mass movement, then planners have to find another way to express the energy of that liturgy. This can even be seen as a positive challenge—how to adapt all our local rites so that they really take life from our common meeting space.

Preparing Persons

While the above forms of pre-liturgy work allow for a wide variety of volunteers, there is still one more field for full involvement. Here the catechists, parents, and youth leaders take a most active role in worship. Preparing liturgically active persons is more than training readers, acolytes, and other such ministers. The whole assembly needs ever more foundation for prayer.

DMC chapter one is entitled "The Introduction of Children to the Eucharistic Celebration." There the most difficult work in children's liturgy is elaborated. The work of planning a Sunday service is far easier than the long-term formation of Christians within the heritage of common prayer.

Carefully structured rites will be hollow unless children grow in and appreciate these human values: "activity of the community, exchange of greetings,
capacity to listen and to seek and grant pardon, expression of gratitude,
experience of symbolic actions, a meal of friendship, and festive celebration"
(DMC, 9). While we consider the mammoth task of sharing these ideals, we
recognize that this is just the beginning. The priming of persons for common
prayer—especially Eucharist—is also an unveiling of faith, guidance in private prayer, and awakening the sense that we are in Christ.

Priorities

Most of these nine forms of liturgy planning exist in every local church.
Readers intent on providing better, more vital, and faith-filled celebrations
should evaluate the "de facto" priorities of parish time. Within planning,
which of these nine receives the most time? Which are ignored? Then some
rechanneling of energies might be considered.

The most common complaint from liturgy committees is that their pastor
will not allow x, y, or z, while xyz is precisely what they want to do. Short
of reaffiliating with another church or causing the pastor to be reassigned,
there exists the possibility of someone's mind being changed. Part of this same
political scene is the advice to choose one's battles. If xyz are impossible, or
if the planning forms above are withheld from the laity, there are still
possibilities for creative and fruitful involvement. Working on environment
and preparing persons for worship are not secondary activities to which
frustrated planners are relegated. This is not an "apologia" for uncooperative
pastors, but a simple statement of fact—there are many long-term ways to
prepare liturgies for children and adults.

The above planning forms are obviously applicable to both general parish
and specific children's liturgies. All these levels should exist in a parish effort
to enable youth to participate more fully. In most cases the work for children
should not exist separate from adult assembly work. "Doing something for
the kids" probably means that we must do something for the whole parish.
Thus the energies of children's liturgy workers should be in close collaboration with other liturgical priorities. A specific children's liturgy committee
may only be necessary for planning specific liturgies on an ad hoc basis for
children's assemblies. Annual, seasonal, and ongoing planning should probably find the children's liturgy advocates at the same meetings with other
parish ministers.

The Meeting Process

When planning a specific liturgy, the first step is forming the planning
group. The 7:00 A.M. service may be planned by the presider alone using the
SOP. The Easter Vigil will probably involve a lot more planners. A particular

children's liturgy would involve a standing committee of parents, catechists, and liturgical ministers or it could be an ad hoc group with the same type mix.

Parallel to the recruitment of planners, someone must schedule a session to adapt the SOP and/or to create a whole new pattern for a unique festival. Quite obviously, it must be early enough to implement any decisions and carefully set so that the right people can be there with undivided attention. Thus the charting of the 7:00 A.M. prayers and homily may take place at the pastor's desk the previous evening. Easter Vigil discussions may begin in January around a large conference table. The children's liturgy for All Saints/ Halloween might be outlined in early October.

An essential but often overlooked facet of scheduling the meeting is setting a reasonable agenda. This begins with a basic question about local ecclesial power: Who sets the agenda and limits? Whether it be the clergy, liturgy coordinators, music directors, or school principal, they should include common prayer in the meeting. In most cases they should provide for some education of the planners (on the feast's universal history, on its local traditions, on unique conditions surroundings this year's celebration). Finally, the meeting initiators should gather the materials which will inform the decision makers: copy any set scripture selections, list any peculiar features of that feast's SOP rites, and collect resource books and props. Some of this material can be mailed to participants early or used for homework between meetings (if this liturgy requires two sessions). The guiding principle is that plans should be made by informed people who can follow a logical agenda.

The meeting itself can be divided into two halves. Part One begins with opening prayer and it should be more than a group recitation of set formulas. The readings preassigned for the feast might be read with sufficient silence. A seasonal hymn might be sung. Then the group can reflect on and discuss the "givens" for that feast—scriptures, community mood, climate, local traditions, fond memories associated with the festival, ministerial resources available, time of the service, and elements that simply must be integrated (e.g. collection). During this phase of discussion decisions about the actual liturgy are put off. This is the time for brainstorming, sharing convictions and general hopes for the event. In this way all participants can get a sense of the feast before engaging in debate over minute elements. If this discussion goes long enough, some consensus should be reached about the tone, thrust, general outline, and/or theme.

After a break, Part Two allows the group to chart out this liturgy's details. In an ad hoc group, where some are liturgical veterans and others are new (and apprehensive about the process), this part may see more input from the people who know ritual language. If the others have been truly heeded in Part One, then they should not feel disenfranchised as they assume an apprentice role for Part Two. The details discussion can usually begin with the congregation's entrance and prelude music then move step by step to the exit and postlude music. From time to time an unusual liturgy will suggest that planners first line up the central part of the rite or the unusual part. Then the other parts may fall into place better and the central event will be ritualized as the key moment. For example, plans for a baptism within the Eucharist may begin by planning the immersion rite and the eucharistic prayer. Then other elements will be added later. On a most practical level, this also insures that the key parts are planned while there is still energy left in the planners.

No matter where in the rite this discussion begins, the process is one of adapting the SOP, even if it's just a very general one (gather, then Word, then sacrament, then depart). The group secretary or every participant should have an easily formulated work sheet. This paper can have three columns: ritual flow, ministers to affect this, and necessary props or artifacts. For a typical Sunday Eucharist the first entry in each column would then be: congregation enters/ushers greet and assist in seating/music background . . . ushers, musicians . . . musical instruments, worship aids/programs. A representative entry for the moment of Infant Baptism would be: baptismal immersion/sung "Amen" by all . . . baptizer, infant, parents, godparents, song leader . . . font filled with warm water, towels, table for drying and dressing infant. The more complete the listings, the easier will be the next step.

After the meeting, someone must carry out the decisions. Who will arrange for the ministers listed in column two? Who will get the items in column three? How will the outline be translated from ink to celebration? This is so important that some churches add a fourth column to the work sheet. There the names of people assuming responsibility for post-meeting arrangements are added. The most sensitive part of this process is communication with important ministers who were absent. If the presider, homilist, or musicians miss this meeting, they must receive a full report conveying the whole flow of the discussion. This is vastly different from mailing an outline to them mandating their chores.

Separate Liturgies?

This planning outline and all of the above processes work for any liturgical assembly—adults or children. A basic decision within the parish's review of worship preparation is whether to split children off from adults. The structure of most families and parishes seem to dictate a normal pattern of full assembly gatherings. Yet there can still be appropriate times for specific groups—children, or adolescents, or neighborhoods. The regular Sunday meeting of the whole parish can benefit from the variety of separate liturgies of the Word with all reassembling for Eucharist. When done well, this meets both the need for unified praise and for opening the Word in comprehensible terms. The DMC suggests,

> It will perhaps be appropriate, if the physical arrangements and the circumstances of the community permit, to celebrate the liturgy of the word, including a homily, with the children in a separate area that is not too far removed. Then, before the eucharistic liturgy begins, the children are led to the place where the adults have meanwhile been celebrating their own liturgy of the word. (#17)

This generally works best if everyone assembles for the opening rites, then those groups of children with special liturgies of the Word leave with their respective leaders. From time to time, separate Word services can be held for every grade level (if there are eight different rooms). Or each week a different age (e.g., grades four and five) has a special service (if there is only one side room). In any event, a common opening rite puts the divided Word liturgies within the clear context of common prayer. This tone must be continued within all the rooms, for these are liturgies of the Word, not religious education classes.

The timing of the assembly reunion is crucial for a prayerful atmosphere. The children should not meander through the church, back to their parents, during the homily or the general intercessions' silence. They should return when the action is appropriate. The children's prayer leaders will want to know how much time they have and the adult assembly homilist/presider must be conscious of the same time flow. One of many possible solutions is for an acolyte to leave the adult assembly as soon as the homily is over, alerting the children's leaders by some prearranged signal. Meanwhile, those leaders have had some general notion of the time frame, with a flexible-length response activity placed at the end of their Word liturgies. When the signal comes they have time to close this action and go to the church vestibule. They can then reenter at the next apt moment—usually during the altar's preparation for Eucharist. Because of this flow, the distinct liturgies of the Word will seem disjointed unless they prayerfully lead the young participants to the point of wanting to give thanks. Then the transition to eucharistic thanks is of one piece.

This is but one variant on the standard ritual. The rites of our churches offer as many adaptations as there are creative, prayerful planners. The key to resolving liturgical frustration is not complaint and protest. The solution lies in long-term preparation, careful analysis of the local church's planning structures, and gradual upgrading of the SOP. This may seem a far cry from spontaneous prayer of the Spirit. Yet we are not angels. We are humans living in complex communities with varied expectations. The work of planning, organization, and pattern analysis is not anti-Spirit. It is a real spiritual ministry.

13

The Pre-schooler in the Liturgy
Gail Ramshaw Schmidt

A friend of mine believes that young children ought to be barred from art museums. He says their running through the galleries belittles art in their eyes, teaches them nothing, and disturbs those who come seriously to view the museum. Even when unspoken, this logic infects our Sunday morning worship patterns in such common practices as seating children in the back row where they can't see a thing; banishing three-, four- or even five-year olds to a cry room for the hour; scheduling a nursery playtime or even Sunday school simultaneously with the liturgy; and neglecting to prepare the children for, and discuss with them afterwards, the order, feeling, and intent of liturgical action. At worst, we simply leave the children at home. These actions imply that children are too young to participate meaningfully in the liturgy, that they are intellectually immature and unable to control their behavior. Children disturb the adults who can participate, understand, and behave.

These arguments are specious in their evaluation of pre-school children and in their understanding of Christian liturgy. Studies now demonstrate what some parents and teachers have always observed: that from infancy through the pre-school years, the human child is a voracious receiver of stimuli; and that the child's consciousness is alive with a fantasy life constituted in great part by the images which are given to encompass that child. An appreciation of the fullness of the interweaving of images and actions of the liturgy would lead us to conclude that young children belong in church as much as any adult.

The decision to bring the pre-schooler to church ought not rest on some current psychological theory. The history of the church's liturgy is a series of an existing practice finding support in contemporary intellectual theory; subsequently the theory becomes prolegomenon for the practice! For example, Protestantism has grounded the age of confirmation and/or communion in the theories of the "age of reason." Even though psychological studies of early childhood stages may highlight significant data, we begin at God's grace.

God's grace: we cannot fathom it. We can say that grace is always bigger than when we first believed, always attends the least of God's little ones, and always defies our definitions about human acceptability. Even if we had no demonstrable evidence that children "got anything out of church," even if they screeched and squirmed for the entire hour every week, our theology of God's grace and our belief in the gift of that grace to the whole Church would ensure our bringing all pre-schoolers to worship every week.

A commercial break, for several stories of children I know:

The eighteen-month-old boy sat up and laughed aloud when the Old Testament lector read about the stem of Jesse. The boy's name is Jesse.

A three-year-old was holding her book open during the reading of Psalm 148. In the moment's silence after verse 7, she exclaimed loud and clear for all to hear, "*Sea* monsters?!"

On Holy Cross Sunday, the child who normally drew flowers all over her bulletin drew instead rows and rows of crosses.

After Sunday liturgy, two toddlers pranced around the chancel with service books in their arms calling out, "Holy Holy. Son Holy Spirit. Hosanna. Son Holy Spirit."

At the *Sursum Corda,* the two-year-old stepped out into the aisle, struck a fine *orans* position, and began rather too loudly to chant the preface.

The four-year-old was persistent: What were the names of the babies to be baptized today? During the sermon she lay down on the pew and covered her head with her coat, the better to suck her thumb peacefully. Five minutes into the sermon the pastor mentioned the babies' names, and she snapped to attention and said, "Mark and Abigail."

Commercial break over.

Liturgy: Growth in Faith

Martin Luther was concerned that the liturgy be a vehicle through which the faithful would grow by learning about the faith. Some of Luther's liturgical reforms demonstrate his interest in this educative aspect of worship. For example, he adapted Latin chants into vernacular, metrical hymns, easy for all to sing. According to the understanding of this time and culture, and in line with his own predilections as a German university professor, he saw the sermon as an essential pedagogical tool within the liturgy. Luther even adapted the offices of morning and evening prayer to make them preaching services for the instruction of the laity.

If we assume that what is to be learned in the liturgy is theology and that it is to be taught by lecture, we would agree that toddlers have little place in such a setting. However, the university lecture is no longer used as the model for the sermon; it is no longer perceived as the most effective way to do liturgy. We do not lecture children about the meaning of birthday parties before we give them a party, neither do we wait until they are able to understand all the facets of the ritual. We place the one-year-old child before a cake and presents, and in the midst of the celebration the child learns what birthday parties are. The Eucharist is the Thanksgiving dinner: the family of God sharing the meal, rehearsing the images of the past, and becoming themselves bearers of the promise.

Despite what preachers in the past thought about the value of lengthy sermons, what we "learn" in the liturgy is not a set of facts but a way of life. Worshipping is the way of life for God's redeemed, it is that simple. The kingdom is lived, the people are washed, the meal is shared, and God is glorified. The pattern is learned in early childhood and rehearsed until death; yet it is known fully only in the end time around the throne of God. And on this side of understanding is the Church: smart people, dull people, doubters, theologians, the senile, the retarded, and the toddlers.

The liturgy teaches by immersing us into a juxtaposition of images, stories, and symbols of the faith. Here is a paschal candle, there a green chasuble, now the angels lauding Christ's birth; and later the people yelling Hosanna. Some liturgical readings were written millenia ago, but they are mingled with hymns composed centuries ago and prayers drafted yesterday. Some themes recur—grace, forgiveness, life—while others are momentary and fragmentary on any particular Sunday. Perhaps Sesame Street took the Sunday liturgy for its model: friendly faces on a family set weaving in short segments an hour of story and song around the day's focus.

This mingling of imagery makes the liturgy accessible to small children whose fantasy life has not yet been tied down by the bonds of analytic logic. Tuning in and out of the liturgy, small children can immediately grab a floating image and fly with it or remember it the next day in private reverie and creative play. It would be instructive to videotape children playing church. I know a child who communed at two and played church at three by handing crackers to each of his dolls while solemnly declaiming, "Grace Lutheran Church. Grace Lutheran Church." One of the many problems inherent in what are sometimes called "children's liturgies" is that the stories, rituals, and images are so watered down that there is no taste left. A story told without the details is not engrossing; a ritual enacted without intentionality is hollow. These images should be allowed to blossom in their naturally wild and colorful profusion so that they will thrive in the children's imaginations. The carefully arranged bouquet on the textbook or floriculture can come later.

Liturgy: The Fear and Love of God

When Luther wrote up the Ten Commandments in "the plain form in which the head of the family shall teach it to his household," he provided explanation to each of the commandments which began with the words, "Wir sollen Gott furchten und lieben." We are to fear and love God. To speak of the dynamics of the liturgy is to say that in worship we fear and love God. Not only love, but also fear: my religion teachers over the years hastened to define fear so that it did not mean fear. But fear is a most appropriate word. If we have not stood in silence and terror before the Almighty, we need not seek refuge in the wounds of Christ. If religion is too comfortable, it has not yet met God.

Children know all about fear. Their perennial fascination with monsters, dinosaurs, nightmares, and fairy tales demonstrates that normally children are alive with awe, filled with fear of the uncontrollable forces of death and life, and comforted by their many rituals of submission and victory. The toddler who asks for a scary story to be told over and over again is establishing a ritual to contain fear and then to conquer it. There is a genuine way in which children tremble with Isaiah before God's throne. The child's fear is grounded in the recognition of otherness, intuitive terror of dependency, and vacillation between horror and fascination of the mighty.

The liturgy should give honest expression to the child's natural fear of the almighty. Where their fear is focused on the evil almighty, children can be redirected to see the pious and saintly fear of the good almighty of God. The three-year-old reported to his mother, who asked what the conversation was about, "We're talking that God is bigger than the monsters." The liturgy need not flinch about death. In one of Sesame Street's weakest moments, Bob sings a laundered version of "I know an old woman who swallowed a fly"; Bob's refrain is, "I think she'll cry." To this a boy in the peanut gallery called out, "No, it's 'I think she'll *die.*'" Poor Bob mumbled something and went on with the song. Children are less afraid of fear than are adults.

Our liturgy can be a vehicle of this primal fear of the unknown. Despite the current emphasis on churches as hospitable houses of God's people, our sanctuaries should not be such commonplace rooms that they call forth no awe from within us. My two-year-old talked for several days about the rose window at the Cathedral of St. John the Divine, just as her older sister had exclaimed for a week about the wall of window at the Metropolitan Museum's Temple of Dendur exhibit. But, alas, our parish church has nothing of this quality.

Dressing up especially for church helps children realize the significance of the event. Remember that King Babar gives his elephants not only useful tools for living but also extravagant outfits for Sunday celebrations. Strict codes of behavior help symbolize for the child that the house of God is a holy place where everything is altered in meeting almighty God. Talking with children about the presence of God, the reality of death, the power of God's washing, the wonder of the Lord's meal, and the promise of the resurrection can focus their religious awe on the fundamentals of the faith.

As Luther knew, the complement to fear is love. If children come upon religious fear naturally, it is their Baptism and our rearing them in that Baptism which gathers them into God's love. The gospel and we as gospel-bearers enlighten the children into life, carrying them into God's embrace and nursing them with God's sweet warm milk so they can face the dark encircled and filled by grace. The liturgy ought to absorb children into its rich texture, just as the richness of the liturgical experience ought to be a paradigm for the wealth of life within God's kingdom. Alexander Schmemann writes, "The aim of religious education . . . is to bring the individual into the life of the church . . . In the past the catechumens were first brought into the church gathering, and only then the meaning, the joy, and the purpose of this gathering was explained to them . . . *Lex orandi lex est credendi.*"[1]

There are ways in which our worship can be more loving to small children. Our strict codes of behavior are balanced by our understanding that healthy children do not sit motionless for an hour. Even the youngest children can be taught how to participate in corporate liturgy. Do all the children, toddlers included, have their own service books, hymnals, and bulletins? The fact that children cannot read is no reason to deprive them of participating by holding their own books. If the toddlers mutilate the books, teach them that, "This is a holy book, it is for praying," or buy them books of their own. Take the effort to keep them always on the right page. Small children delight in complicated rules and elaborate procedures, and are proud to join in the pattern. Recall that children walking down the sidewalk make up rules about not stepping on the lines. If there is a choice, provide traditional pews for the children to sit on: they like to lie down, and to stand on the kneelers.

Older children can be trained as lectors to hand out bulletins and take up the offering. Children serving as acolytes need not merely fiddle with the candles, but can assist the presiding minister in significant ways. The older children in such roles provide inspiring models for those younger. In some churches, children tune in only at candle-lighting and at baptisms, for only there are human beings their size involved. At baptisms the younger children can gather around the font. The perturbation of the godparents who feel upstaged is less important than the opportunity to involve children in this central Christian act.

Children's choirs can sing not extraneous ditties but liturgical chants, perhaps the offertory verse. There can be a short children's homily if the presider is capable of making explicit the links between the images in the lessons or the symbols of the season with the Church's sacramental life. For example, on "You are the light of the world" Sunday, the connection can be made to the paschal candle and to the children's own baptismal candles. Teachers and parents should be encouraged to teach even toddlers the chants of the ordinary as regular songs so that the children can participate long before they can read. My two-year-old asks every night for her favorite song: of the dozens she knows, secular, sacred, and "children's," she asks for "Alleluia" by which she means the eleventh-century Easter sequence hymn. Friends were awakened one night by their toddler whimpering, "Daddy, daddy!" He answered, "What?" and she cried out, "Daddy, sing Lamb of God!"

Similarly, Bible stories taught in religious classes are not merely isolated historical narratives or examples of manners and morals, but vehicles into the liturgy. Noah's ark games can be linked with Baptism. The dinner at Emmaus is a picture of the Eucharist. The *Sanctus* can be taught as a goodnight hymn—the angels praising God and so keeping the monsters away. Hearing the introduction to the story of Moses in the bulrushes, the four-year old interrupted: "Why, that's just like Jesus, he had a bad king who killed the baby boys and he went to Egypt . . . ." The children can assemble the puzzle if we point them towards the pieces.

I know an adult who can trace her dread that the good things in life are not for her to having been deprived of Holy Communion as a small child. She vividly recalls her feelings of rejection. There is no better way for children to be embraced by the liturgy, community, and God, than for them to commune. While the piety bolstering our rationalizations concerning communion age may last for many decades, we are now having to admit that the arguments offered over the centuries—the scrupulous concern for the literalness of the body and blood, emphasis on the church's penitential system, and the modern stress on human reason and book learning—are invalid.

To preach the centrality of the Eucharist while denying it to children ignores the fact that a person's most profound and abiding attitudes about life are formed during the earliest pre-verbal years. It is not that one has many specific memories from pre-school years, but that the very categories into which future experience fits are formulated during the first few years of life. The meal, Luther reminds us, is *pro me*. It is not just, as I heard quipped, that "if there's anything kids understand, it's food." It is rather that the love of God passes all understanding; it is a gift to the baptized. The liturgy is to surround children with God's nurturing love, and catechetical instruction can later supply to that embrace the correct theological labels.

Liturgy: Home Ritual

Another of Luther's hobbyhorses provides a final consideration. Luther's insistence that Christian education be a responsibility of the head of the household cannot be ignored quietly as if it were a remnant from simpler times. To romanticize the households of Luther's day is foolish; to despair over the households of today is to demonstrate a lack of faith. Christian education in the home will not likely take the form of group recitations. But for children to make the connections in the liturgy, the data must be increasingly familiar. The stories must be told, the symbols explained, the hymns sung, the themes recalled, and the saints remembered. Breakfast can begin, "O Lord, open my lips," "And my mouth shall declare your praise." The Sunday liturgy, major festivals, and liturgical symbols require the same instructional background, comment, and review which the family and culture afford to Santa Claus, the Easter Bunny, Valentine's Day, and Halloween. Is it Lent? Then note the purple chasuble, and dress the child in purple. We have at least made a beginning when a sixteen-month-old child goes to church on Palm Sunday babbling about "pom-poms."

When our regular experience falls short of all these glorious ideals, we ought to figure out why. The fault may lie with stodgy liturgical practice, inhospitable presiders, insufficient catechetical instruction, unfortunate architecture, or tired parents. Sunday school materials imply that being a Christian is about being good. However, if going to church is about being good, and it is hard for children to "be good," it is difficult for children to connect themselves with church. If, on the other hand, the Christian life is about our claiming a tradition of images of faith as our own, about fearing and loving God, and about being baptized and fed, then children are ready to share in life.

What may be hidden in our tendency to shelter children from the power of liturgy is our own doubts about the life of worship. It is when we weary of our country that we do not take our children to the Fourth of July parade. Is it true equally that we keep them from the *Sanctus* because we are perplexed by the angels? When accepting his Nobel Prize, Isaac Bashevis Singer said of children, "They still believe in good, the family, angels, devils, witches, goblins, logic, clarity, punctuation, and other such obsolete stuff." What may be involved is our bringing the children along to church as they bring us back to faith. It is the two-year-old who climbs up on his parents' bed to bring the cross down from the wall, and processes through the house, holding high the cross and singing "Alleluia." To such belong the kingdom of heaven.

NOTE

1. Alexander Schmemann, *Liturgy and Life: Christian Development through Liturgical Experience* (Syosset, NY: Orthodox Church in America, 1974).

14

Children at Worship:
A Presbyterian Perspective
Virginia Thomas

Presbyterian children and Presbyterian worship are an uneasy combination. In theology they belong together; in practice their association is questionable.

Consider the children. Through their first decade of life physical activity is both a necessity and a primary avenue of learning. They use every sense to acquire concrete knowledge of their world. They focus attention intently, but indiscriminately. Only in the later years of childhood do they begin to organize this accumulation of information into concepts. They are emotional barometers, registering the "feel" of events and environment even when meaning is beyond them.

Now consider Presbyterian worship. It is primarily a verbal, mental experience. In seeking to be true to the Reformed emphasis on participation with understanding, Presbyterians have made this corporate response primarily intellectual. Maintaining the centrality of God's Word in scripture and sermon has resulted in the necessity for a good vocabulary and a disciplined attention span. The liturgy is weighted with abstract words and profound concepts. Mindful of Paul's injunction to do all things decently and in order, we control both motion and emotion.

These considerations are incomplete, of course. At any stage of development children need the love, forgiveness, and wholeness the words of the gospel convey. These words are spoken and even demonstrated in Presbyterian worship. God does speak to us in words and the comprehending of these words. Through the Spirit's enabling action our liturgy can be the occasion of God's coming to children of all ages and lifting them to a response of love and praise.

Nevertheless, these two descriptions do reflect the tension between Presbyterian corporate worship and the developing child. We have never reconciled the strong emphasis on intellectual understanding in worship with the way children understand. The character and form of Presbyterian liturgy almost defines participation in a way that guarantees children cannot participate.

Does this mean we should change worship to fit children? Can this be done with integrity and faithfulness to our interpretation of the Bible? Or should we adapt the children to fit the liturgy? Should we encourage an amicable separation? A separate experience for children? Do we ignore the tension? Ignore the children? Or do we optimistically assume children will inevitably come to worship some day whatever the case may be now?

In practice, Presbyterians have given all of these answers. Measured by our theological standards, however, few of these approaches are acceptable. Before we can fairly judge existing practices regarding children and worship, we need to examine the theology relating to these questions.

Presbyterian theology strongly affirms the church membership of children of believing parents (*Book of Order*, 36–02) and the nurturing responsibility of the worshipping congregation. This is the theological basis for the inclusion of children in corporate worship.

In baptizing an infant we recognize God's prior action and welcome the child into the household of faith. The sacrament speaks the same word whether administered to children or adults. We confirm the love of a sovereign God for this child, the work of Christ in behalf of this child, and the presence of the Spirit in the life of this child.

As a member of the Body of Christ, this child is called to glorify and enjoy God in a life of worship, and in worship with the gathered congregation. The call to worship is not given with minimum age requirements.

Membership in the Body of Christ is also a call to ministry. We are to share the gifts of Christ for the mutual good of all the saints (*Confession of Faith*, Ch. 28:1). Infants and children are included in this call to ministry, though adults are slow to recognize and appreciate the gifts the young have to share. The simple presence of the infant in Baptism may be our clearest testimony to the unmerited grace of God. The trust of a toddler with a parent in worship may speak God's word more effectively than any sermon. This call to ministry will surely be obeyed in the worshipping congregation as well as the world.

The Baptism of a child is also a dramatic statement about the Church. The sacrament is not the isolated experience of one individual. Rather, it is an experience of and within the covenant community. Parental and congregational vows are taken which demonstrate our relation to one another and this child in Christ.

Both parent(s) and congregation are assuming responsibilities in Baptism that can only be fulfilled in "humble reliance on divine grace." Parents promise to pray with and for the child, to instruct the child, and to strive by all the means of God's appointment to nurture the child. The congregation, as one part of the universal Church, stands with the parent(s) to signify the assumption of nurturing responsibility (*Book of Church Order*, "Directory for Worship," 209–5).

Nurturing is a much broader concept than simply education. It means including experiences, offering models, and ministering to emotional and physical needs.

Now the purpose of worship is not the nurture of children but the adoration of God. Yet worship is a nurturing experience. One offering in worship may well be our welcome and nurture of God's children in the sanctuary. If the worship of the Church is the central, identifying act of God's people, it is difficult to imagine nurturing a child without inclusion in this experience.

The call of all members to worship and ministry places baptized children with the congregation at worship. The parental and congregational responsibility to nurture constrains us to welcome them to the corporate service. This nurturing responsibility, while specifically assumed for baptized children, also includes all children for whom the Church has care.

Turning from the theological rationale for children at worship, we will note briefly theology and polity affecting worship. Neither service book nor prescribed liturgy dictate Presbyterian worship. While the way we respond in worship is based on Reformed biblical interpretation, there is no single, correct form. Our standards of doctrine and polity instruct us to assemble, sing hymns and psalms, pray, listen obediently to scripture and sermon, make offerings, and administer the sacraments (*Book of Church Order*, "Directory for Worship," 202–1). Public worship is not complete without the Word read and preached. The visible Word of the Lord's Supper may occur as infrequently as once a quarter. Both the ordering of the acts of worship and the frequency of communion celebration are determined by the Session (elders) of each local church.

In practice, churches do develop fixed orders of worship with the Lord's Prayer and some responses, such as the Doxology, repeated every Sunday. Some churches follow the services of *The Worshipbook*. All churches use a hymnbook, although not necessarily one published by the denomination. A printed order of worship or worship bulletin is the rule rather than the exception. A participant can become familiar with a service through repetition, but almost all public worship requires the ability to read the bulletin, printed prayers, and hymns.

Naturally, worship is not limited to the public assembling of the congregation. Christians are called to worship in all times and places, in private and in families. Yet we always worship as part of the Body of Christ and this worship is an extension of corporate worship. When families do worship at home, the acts and ordering of public worship somehow make "sense" to a kindergarten or elementary school child.

The PCUS constitution directs children to sit with their families in public worship (BCO, DFW, 203–4). There are no such specific directives about age for or ways of including children in the public service. Parents, bearing primary responsibility, make such decisions when and if they are intentionally made. Churches naturally affect these decisions by their policies of child-care and education.

We look at church policies first.

In small rural churches, children are simply present from infancy on. Space and available leadership limit other options, though apparently few consider other options desirable. In a comfortable, informal atmosphere all ages are together with care being given to children as need arises. From birth to youth children observe adults, imitate, take part as they can, and learn by repetition. We should observe here that informality does not necessarily mean careless liturgy.

In a larger suburban or city setting there will be a different scheme for inclusion. A nursery and/or educational experience is offered for pre-school children during the hour for worship. Some congregations continue an extended educational hour during worship for children through early elementary grades. Other churches, by lack of such program for elementary children, imply that they are to join with the rest of the congregation in worship at this age. Only occasionally does a young elementary school child come to worship without an older member of the family or some adult friend.

In some churches, pre-school and elementary-school children are present for the first part of the worship service. They leave before the scripture and sermon for study and play. In this pattern of inclusion, a children's sermon or object lesson may be given before the children leave. These are apt to be moral talks rather than the proclamation of the gospel.

Even when children remain through the entire service, they may be called to the front of the sanctuary to listen to a talk directed to them. These messages are growing in popularity as a way to include young Christians in worship. To this writer's knowledge there has been no serious effort to evaluate how this practice contributes to a child's understanding of worship or to test it by the central role of the Word of God in Reformed worship.

In the South, children, youth, and often adults study in graded church-school classes for an hour, then join together for corporate worship in the sanctuary. This pattern, still followed in many Southern Presbyterian churches, began to change following the Second World War. Rapidly growing churches required double or multiple services, one of which always coincided with church school. Parents had the easy option of worshipping while children were studying. New residents from other parts of the country were familiar with this one-hour worship or study practice more common outside the South. After the need for several services was gone, the practice remained in force.

A strong church-school or Sunday-school program may become a substitute for corporate worship. Ironically, children could study the meaning of worship at each level of the curriculum cycle without ever being a part of a congregational worship service.

Some churches choose as a deliberate policy to keep children from the sanctuary regularly until the time of confirmation. Recognizing the problem children have with Presbyterian liturgy, they deem it best for both young and old to be separate during worship. Church school or a junior church service is planned as an alternative to worship with the congregation in these situations. There is certainly no law that an elementary-school child may not come to worship, but it takes raw courage on the part of a parent or a very docile child to oppose both practice and scheduling.

One way churches of many sizes and strategies incorporate children in worship is through a graded choir program. A junior choir may contribute music each Sunday if there are two services, or perhaps once a month, or perhaps only on festival occasions. A choir program can mean children learn responses, hymns, the order of worship, and choral music as preparation for worship leadership. It can also mean only that children are learning to perform special music. A subtle attitude may develop which says, "I come to worship because I am a member of a choir" rather than "I come to worship because I am a Christian."

Church policies direct parents, and parents shape church policies. However, in the matter of participation in worship, parents are the determining factor, and the participation of children in worship indicates something of the values and attitudes of the parents. Some parents assume children are to worship just as any Christian does, and they simply take their children to worship. Children's assumptions generally match their parents'. A large number of parents think worship for children is a good idea in theory and a disaster in practice when the children sit with them. Some feel worship is a good option if the child freely chooses it. And others are convinced that corporate worship is an adult activity, detrimental to children before adolescence. All of these understandings are held by professing Christian parents whose children have been baptized.

The dominant impression of local church practice is of strategies springing from relative indifference, tolerant acceptance, or definite opposition to children in the assembled congregation. Parental practice is based on both convenience and convictions. There is a wide divergence in how baptismal vows are fulfilled.

When we consider the difficulties Presbyterian worship presents to those of pre-school and elementary ages it is not surprising that churches and parents have responded in such a mixed—and often counter-productive—fashion to the question of children's place at worship. What is surprising, in a church that accepts the covenant theology of birth and growth in Jesus Christ rather than dramatic conversion to him, is how many parents and leaders expect some dramatic conversion to corporate worship apart from instruction, models, practice, or persuasion.

Early adolescence is a time when many youth choose to be confirmed in their church membership, or, for those who have been nurtured toward believer's Baptism (an option on equal footing with the Infant Baptism in the UPCUSA Church), to join the church. At this age the young persons may also be choosing to worship rather than study in church school, reflecting a new understanding of worship, boredom in church school, or a desire to appear more adult. In any case, they take the step into adult, governing membership of the church with very limited experience in congregational worship.

A number of trends and events in the past decade have caused Presbyterians to look carefully at both our children and our worship. One such trend is decreasing attendance of both children and adults in worship. Contemporary liturgical expressions have pushed us to distinguish between what is scriptural and what is custom. A generation of church members raised with television hear music and sermons in a different way. A secular culture claims Sunday, once set apart for worship, as just another day.

Church education has felt the impact of educational research, opening new understandings of how children develop socially and mentally. Such knowledge sheds new light on how children can participate in worship and what our expectations may be. Such research seems to confirm that experience in worship must precede understanding of worship.

The single event that has stimulated the most intense examination of practice and policy has been the change in the constitutional standards to admit baptized children to the Lord's Table. (In 1971 for the UPCUSA. In 1980 for the PCUS.) For several hundred years Reformed and Presbyterian churches have, in a strangely inconsistent fashion, welcomed baptized infants into the church, and excluded them from Communion until Confirmation.

The unspoken idea of a "sub-standard" membership for baptized children implied in the exclusion from the sacrament was demolished in polity if not completely in congregational consciousness. More significantly, this renewed understanding of children as full members helped turn attention to their capabilities and contributions rather than to their limitations.

Since Presbyterian worship never divorces the Lord's Supper from the spoken Word, it has been imperative for us to look at this experience through the eyes of a child. There are possibilities here for a sharpened use of words, more concrete images, a renewed emphasis on the dramatic storytelling of biblical narrative, and illustrative material and applications that include many ages. The sermon may become God's Word to everyone, rather than a dividing line between children and adults.

The Lord's Supper is, except in the case of invalids or very unusual circumstances, an experience of corporate worship. (Even in these cases, it is an extension of corporate worship.) Hence, we must look at worship as a child sees worship. Such a viewpoint helps us realize the value of color, drama, movement, and spontaneity. It protects us from confusing austerity with integrity, formality with reverence, and theological depth with obscurity.

Looking at the sacrament as children do, we have been forced to consider unfamiliar meanings that are equally valid and enriching. The Presbyterian emphasis on repentance and worthy participation has been expanded to include the equally biblical themes of thanksgiving, community, and celebration, themes that speak to our younger members. Our highly cognitive approach must be modified to recognize that not all understanding is intellectual.

Because parents are involved directly—or indirectly—in this inclusion of baptized children in the Lord's Supper, we have been compelled to take seriously our congregational vow to support them in nurture. Educational ventures aiding them to prepare themselves and their children in worship and the Sacrament have reinforced them in their role and reminded them their children are truly members of the worshipping community.

In short, by taking seriously the place of children in this visible Word at the heart of our worship, we have the possibility for invigorating, theologically sound ways of making worship meaningful to Christians of all ages.

Appendix One
Directory for Masses with Children

INTRODUCTION

1. The Church shows special concern for baptized children who have yet to be fully initiated through the sacraments of confirmation and eucharist as well as for children who have only recently been admitted to holy communion. Today the circumstances in which children grow up are not favorable to their spiritual progress.[1] In addition, sometimes parents barely fulfill the obligations of Christian education which they undertake at the baptism of their children.

2. In bringing up children in the Church a special difficulty arises from the fact that liturgical celebrations, especially the eucharist, cannot fully exercise their innate pedagogical force upon children.[2] Although the mother tongue may now be used at Mass, still the words and signs have not been sufficiently adapted to the capacity of children.

In fact, even in daily life children cannot always understand everything that they experience with adults, and they easily become weary. It cannot be expected, moreover, that everything in the liturgy will always be intelligible to them. Nonetheless, we may fear spiritual harm if over the years children repeatedly experience in the Church things that are scarcely comprehensible to them: recent psychological study has established how profoundly children are formed by the religious experience of infancy and early childhood, according to their individual religious capacity.[3]

3. The Church follows its Master, who "put his arms around the children . . . and blessed them" (Mark 10:16). It cannot leave children to themselves. The Second Vatican Council had spoken in the Constitution on the Liturgy about the need of liturgical adaptation for various groups.[4] Soon afterwards, especially in the first Synod of Bishops held in Rome in 1967, the Church began to consider how participation of children could be made easier. On the occasion of the Synod the president of the Consilium for the Implementation of the Constitution on the Liturgy said explicitly that it could not be a matter of "creating some entirely special rite but rather of retaining, shortening, or omitting some elements or of making a better selection of texts."[5]

4. All the details of eucharistic celebration with a congregation were determined in the General Instruction of the revised *Roman Missal*, published in 1969. Then this congregation began to prepare a special directory for Masses with children, as a supplement to the instruction. This was done in response to repeated petitions from

the entire Catholic world and with the cooperation of men and women specialists from almost every nation.

5. Like the General Instruction, this directory reserves some adaptations to conferences of bishops or individual bishops.[6]

With regard to adaptations of the Mass which may be necessary for children in a given country but which cannot be included in this general directory, the conferences of bishops should submit proposals to the Apostolic See, in accord with article 40 of the Constitution on the Liturgy. These adaptations are to be introduced only with the consent of the Apostolic See.

6. The directory is concerned with children who have not yet entered the period of pre-adolescence. It does not speak directly of children who are physically or mentally retarded because a broader adaptation is sometimes necessary for them.[7] Nevertheless, the following norms may also be applied to the retarded, with the necessary changes.

7. The first chapter of the directory (nos. 8-15) gives a kind of foundation by considering the different ways in which children are introduced to the eucharistic liturgy. The second chapter briefly treats Masses with adults, in which children also take part (nos. 16-19). Finally, the third chapter (nos. 20-54) treats at greater length Masses with children, in which only some adults take part.

CHAPTER I
THE INTRODUCTION OF CHILDREN
TO THE EUCHARISTIC CELEBRATION

8. A fully Christian life cannot be conceived without participation in the liturgical services in which the faithful, gathered into a single assembly, celebrate the paschal mystery. Therefore, the religious initiation of children must be in harmony with this purpose.[8] By baptizing infants, the Church expresses its confidence in the gifts received from this sacrament; thus it must be concerned that the baptized grow in communion with Christ and the brethren. Sharing in the eucharist is the sign and pledge of this very communion. Children are prepared for eucharistic communion and introduced more deeply into its meaning. It is not right to separate such liturgical and eucharistic formation from the general human and Christian education of children. Indeed it would be harmful if liturgical formation lacked such a foundation.

9. For this reason all who have a part in the formation of children should consult and work together. In this way even if children already have some feeling for God and the things of God, they may also experience the human values which are found in the eucharistic celebration, depending upon their age and personal progress. These values are the activity of the community, exchange of greetings, capacity to listen and to seek and grant pardon, expression of gratitude, experience of symbolic actions, a meal of friendship, and festive celebration.[9]

Eucharistic catechesis, which is mentioned in no. 12, should go beyond such human values. Thus, depending on their age, psychological condition, and social situation, children may gradually open their minds to the perception of Christian values and the celebration of the mystery of Christ.[10]

10. The Christian family has the greatest role in teaching these Christian and human values.[11] Thus Christian education, provided by parents and other educators, should be strongly encouraged in relation to liturgical formation of children as well.

By reason of the responsibility freely accepted at the baptism of their children, parents are bound in conscience to teach them gradually to pray. This they do by praying with them each day and by introducing them to prayers said privately.[12] If children are prepared in this way, even from their early years, and do take part in the Mass with their family when they wish, they will easily begin to sing and to pray in the liturgical community, indeed they will have some kind of foretaste of the eucharistic mystery.

If the parents are weak in faith but still wish their children to receive Christian formation, at least they should be urged to share the human values mentioned above with their children. On occasion, they should be encouraged to participate in meetings of parents and in non-eucharistic celebrations with their children.

11. The Christian communities to which the individual families belong or in which the children live also have a responsibility toward children baptized in the Church. By giving witness to the Gospel, living fraternal charity, actively celebrating the mysteries of Christ, the Christian community is the best school of Christian and liturgical formation for the children who live in it.

Within the Christian community, godparents and others with special concern who are moved by apostolic zeal can help greatly in the necessary catechesis of children of families which are unable to fulfill their own responsibility in Christian education.

In particular these ends can be served by preschool programs, Catholic schools, and various kinds of classes for children.

12. Even in the case of children, the liturgy itself always exerts its own proper didactic force.[13] Yet within programs of catechetical, scholastic, and parochial formation, the necessary importance should be given to catechesis on the Mass.[14] This catechesis should be directed to the child's active, conscious, and authentic participation.[15] "Clearly accommodated to the age and mentality of the children, it should attempt, through the principal rites and prayers, to convey the meaning of the Mass, including a participation in the whole life of the Church."[16] This is especially true of the text of the eucharistic prayer and of the acclamations with which the children take part in this prayer.

Special mention should be made of the catechesis through which children are prepared for first communion. Not only should they learn the truths of faith concerning the eucharist, but they should also understand how from first communion on— prepared by penance according to their need and fully initiated into the body of Christ—they may actively participate in the eucharist with the people of God and have their place at the Lord's table and in the community of the brethren.

13. Various kinds of celebrations may also play a major role in the liturgical formation of children and in their preparation for the Church's liturgical life. By the very fact of celebration children easily come to appreciate some liturgical elements, for example, greetings, silence, and common praise (especially when this is sung in common). Such celebrations, however, should avoid having too didactic a character.

14. Depending on the capacity of the children, the word of God should have a greater and greater place in these celebrations. In fact, as the spiritual capacity of children develops, celebrations of the word of God in the strict sense should be held frequently, especially during Advent and Lent.[17] These will help greatly to develop in the children an appreciation of the word of God.

15. Over and above what has been said already, all liturgical and eucharistic formation should be directed toward a greater and greater response to the Gospel in the daily life of the children.

CHAPTER II
MASSES WITH ADULTS IN WHICH CHILDREN ALSO PARTICIPATE

16. Parish Masses are celebrated in many places, especially on Sundays and holydays,

with a large number of adults and a smaller number of children. On such occasions the witness of adult believers can have a great effect upon the children. Adults can also benefit spiritually from experiencing the part which the children have within the Christian community. If children take part in these Masses together with their parents and other members of their family, this should be of great help to the Christian spirit of families.

Infants who as yet are unable or unwilling to take part in the Mass may be brought in at the end of Mass to be blessed together with the rest of the community. This may be done, for example, if parish helpers have been taking care of them in a separate area.

17. Nevertheless, in Masses of this kind it is necessary to take great care that the children do not feel neglected because of their inability to participate or to understand what happens and what is proclaimed in the celebration. Some account should be taken of their presence, for example, by speaking to them directly in the introductory comments (as at the beginning and the end of Mass) and in part of the homily.

Sometimes, moreover, it will perhaps be appropriate, if the physical arrangements and the circumstances of the community permit, to celebrate the liturgy of the word, including a homily, with the children in a separate area that is not too far removed. Then, before the eucharistic liturgy begins, the children are led to the place where the adults have meanwhile been celebrating their own liturgy of the word.

18. It may also be very helpful to give some tasks to the children. They may, for example, bring forward the gifts or sing one or other of the parts of Mass.

19. Sometimes, if the number of children is large, it may be suitable to plan the Masses so that they correspond better to the needs of the children. In this case the homily should be directed to the children but in such a way that adults may also benefit from it. In addition to the adaptations now in the Order of Mass, one or other of the special adaptations described below may be employed in a Mass celebrated with adults in which children also participate, where the bishop permits such adaptations.

CHAPTER III
MASSES WITH CHILDREN IN WHICH
ONLY A FEW ADULTS PARTICIPATE

20. In addition to the Masses in which children take part with their parents and other members of their family (which are not always possible everywhere), Masses with children in which only some adults take part are recommended, especially during the week. From the beginning of the liturgical restoration it has been clear to everyone that some adaptations are necessary in these Masses.[18]

Such adaptations, but only those of a more general kind, will be considered below (nos. 38-54).

21. It is always necessary to keep in mind that through these eucharistic celebrations children must be led toward the celebration of Mass with adults, especially the Masses in which the Christian community comes together on Sundays.[19] Thus, apart from adaptations which are necessary because of the children's age, the result should not be entirely special rites which differ too greatly from the Order of Mass celebrated with a congregation.[20] The purpose of the various elements should always correspond with what is said in the General Instruction of the *Roman Missal* on individual points, even if at times for pastoral reasons an absolute *identity* cannot be insisted upon.

OFFICES AND MINISTRIES IN THE CELEBRATION

22. The principles of active and conscious participation are in a sense even more valid for Masses celebrated with children. Every effort should be made to increase this participation and to make it more intense. For this reason as many children as possible should have special parts in the celebration, for example: preparing the place and the altar (see no. 29), acting as cantor (see no. 24), singing in a choir, playing musical instruments (see no. 32), proclaiming the readings (see nos. 24 and 47), responding during the homily (see no. 48), reciting the intentions of the general intercessions, bringing the gifts to the altar, and performing similar activities in accord with the usage of various communities (see no. 34).

To encourage participation it will sometimes be helpful to have several additions, for example, the insertion of motives for giving thanks before the priest begins the dialogue of the preface.

In all this one should keep in mind that external activities will be fruitless and even harmful if they do not serve the internal participation of the children. Thus religious silence has its importance even in Masses with children (see no. 37). The children should not be allowed to forget that all the forms of participation reach their high point in eucharistic communion when the body and blood of Christ are received as spiritual nourishment.[21]

23. It is the responsibility of the priest who celebrates with children to make the celebration festive, fraternal, meditative.[22] Even more than in Masses with adults, the priest should try to bring about this kind of spirit. It will depend upon his personal preparation and his manner of acting and speaking with others.

Above all, the priest should be concerned about the dignity, clarity, and simplicity of his actions and gestures. In speaking to the children he should express himself so that he will be easily understood, while avoiding any childish style of speech.

The free use of introductory comments[23] will lead children to a genuine liturgical participation, but these explanations should not be merely didactic.

It will help in reaching the hearts of the children if the priest sometimes uses his own words when he gives invitations, for example, at the penitential rite, the prayer over the gifts, the Lord's Prayer, the sign of peace, and communion.

24. Since the eucharist is always the action of the entire Church community, the participation of at least some adults is desirable. These should be present not as monitors but as participants, praying with the children and helping them to the extent necessary.

With the consent of the pastor or the rector of the church, one of the adults may speak to the children after the gospel, especially if the priest finds it difficult to adapt himself to the mentality of the children. In this matter the norms of the Congregation for the Clergy should be observed.

The diversity of ministries should also be encouraged in Masses with children so that the Mass may be evidently the celebration of a community.[24] For example, readers and cantors, whether children or adults, should be employed. In this way variety will keep the children from becoming tired because of the sameness of voices.

PLACE AND TIME OF CELEBRATION

25. The primary place for the eucharistic celebration for children is the church. Within the church, however, a space should be carefully chosen, if available, which will be suited to the number of participants. It should be a place where the children can conduct themselves freely according to the demands of a living liturgy that is suited to their age.

If the church does not satisfy these demands, it will sometimes be suitable to celebrate the eucharist with children outside a sacred place. Then the place chosen should be appropriate and worthy.[25]

26. The time of day chosen for Masses with children should correspond with the circumstances of their lives so that they may be most open to hearing the word of God and to celebrating the eucharist.

27. Weekday Mass in which children participate can certainly be celebrated with greater effect and less danger of weariness if it does not take place every day (for example, in boarding schools). Moreover, preparation can be more careful if there is a longer interval between celebrations.

Sometimes it is preferable to have common prayer to which the children may contribute spontaneously, either a common meditation or a celebration of the word of God. These celebrations continue the eucharist and lead to deeper participation in later eucharistic celebrations.

28. When the number of children who celebrate the eucharist together is very great, attentive and conscious participation becomes more difficult. Therefore, if possible, several groups should be formed; these should not be set up rigidly according to age but with regard to the progress of religious formation and catechetical preparation of the children.

During the week such groups may be invited to the sacrifice of the Mass on different days.

PREPARATION FOR THE CELEBRATION

29. Each eucharistic celebration with children should be carefully prepared beforehand, especially with regard to prayers, songs, readings, and intentions of the general intercessions. This should be done in discussion with the adults and with the children who will have a special ministry in these Masses. If possible, some of the children should take part in preparing and ornamenting the place of celebration and preparing the chalice with the paten and the cruets. Over and above the appropriate internal participation, such activity will help to develop the spirit of community celebration.

SINGING AND MUSIC

30. Singing is of great importance in all celebrations, but it is to be especially encouraged in every way for Masses celebrated with children, in view of their special affinity for music.[26] The culture of various groups and the capabilities of the children present should be taken into account.

If possible the acclamations should be sung by the children rather than recited, especially the acclamations which are a part of the eucharistic prayer.

31. To facilitate the children's participation in singing the Gloria, profession of faith, Sanctus, and Agnus Dei, it is permissible to use music set to appropriate vernacular texts, accepted by the competent authority, even if these do not agree completely with the liturgical texts.[27]

32. The use of "musical instruments may be of great help" in Masses with children, especially if they are played by the children themselves.[28] The playing of instruments will help to support the singing or to encourage the reflection of the children; sometimes by themselves instruments express festive joy and the praise of God.

Care should always be taken, however, that the music does not prevail over the singing or become a distraction rather than a help to the children. Music should correspond to the purpose which is attached to the different periods for which it is introduced into the Mass.

With these precautions and with special and necessary concern, music that is technically produced may be also used in Masses with children, in accord with norms established by the conferences of bishops.

GESTURES AND ACTIONS
33. The development of gestures, postures, and actions is very important for Masses with children in view of the nature of the liturgy as an activity of the entire man and in view of the psychology of children. This should be done in harmony with the age and local usage. Much depends not only on the actions of the priest,[29] but also on the manner in which the children conduct themselves as a community.

If a conference of bishops, in accord with the norm of the General Instruction of the *Roman Missal*,[30] adapts the actions of the Mass to the mentality of the people, it should give consideration to the special condition of children or should determine such adaptations for children only.
34. Among the actions which are considered under this heading, processions deserve special mention as do other activities which involve physical participation.

The processional entrance of the children with the priest may help them to experience a sense of the communion that is thus constituted.[31] The participation of at least some children in the procession with the book of gospels makes clear the presence of Christ who announces his word to the people. The procession of children with the chalice and the gifts expresses clearly the value and meaning of the preparation of gifts. The communion procession, if properly arranged, helps greatly to develop the piety of the children.

VISUAL ELEMENTS
35. The liturgy of the Mass contains many visual elements, and these should be given great prominence with children. This is especially true of the particular visual elements in the course of the liturgical year, for example, the veneration of the cross, the Easter candle, the lights on the feast of the Presentation of the Lord, and the variety of colors and liturgical ornaments.

In addition to the visual elements that belong to the celebration and to the place of celebration, it is appropriate to introduce other elements which will permit children to perceive visually the great deeds of God in creation and redemption and thus support their prayer. The liturgy should never appear as something dry and merely intellectual.
36. For the same reason the use of pictures prepared by the children themselves may be useful, for example, to illustrate a homily, to give a visual dimension to the intentions of the general intercessions, or to inspire reflection.

SILENCE
37. Even in Masses with children "silence should be observed at the proper time as a part of the celebration"[32] lest too great a role be given to external action. In their own way children are genuinely capable of reflection. They need, however, a kind of introduction so that they will learn how to reflect within themselves, meditate briefly, or praise God and pray to him in their hearts,[33] for example after the homily or after communion.[34]

Besides this, with even greater care than in Masses with adults, the liturgical texts should be spoken intelligibly and unhurriedly, with the necessary pauses.

THE PARTS OF MASS

38. The general structure of the Mass, which "in some sense consists of two parts, namely, the liturgy of the word and the liturgy of the eucharist," should always be maintained as should some rites to open and conclude the celebration.[35] Within individual parts of the celebration the adaptations which follow seem necessary if children are truly to experience, in their own way and according to the psychological patterns of childhood, "the mystery of faith . . . by means of rites and prayers."[36]

39. Some rites and texts should never be adapted for children lest the difference between Masses with children and the Masses with adults become too great.[37] These are "the acclamations and the responses of the faithful to the greetings of the priest,"[38] the Lord's Prayer, and the trinitarian formula at the end of the blessing with which the priest concludes the Mass. It is urged, moreover, that children should become accustomed to the Nicene Creed little by little, while the use of the Apostles' Creed mentioned in no. 49 is permitted.

a) **Introductory Rite**

40. The introductory rite of Mass has the purpose "that the faithful, assembling in unity, should constitute a communion and should prepare themselves properly for hearing the word of God and celebrating the eucharist worthily."[39] Therefore every effort should be made to create this disposition in the children and to avoid any excess of rites in this part of Mass.

It is sometimes proper to omit one or other element of the introductory rite or perhaps to enlarge one of the elements. There should always be at least some introductory element, which is completed by the opening prayer or collect. In choosing individual elements one should be careful that each one be used at times and that none be entirely neglected.

b) **Reading and Explanation of the Word of God**

41. Since readings taken from holy scripture constitute "the principal part of the liturgy of the word,"[40] biblical reading should never be omitted even in Masses celebrated with children.

42. With regard to the number of readings on Sundays and feast days, the decrees of the conferences of bishops should be observed. If three or even two readings on Sundays or weekdays can be understood by children only with difficulty, it is permissible to read two or only one of them, but the reading of the gospel should never be omitted.

43. If all the readings assigned to the day seem to be unsuited to the capacity of the children, it is permissible to choose readings or a reading either from the *Lectionary for Mass* or directly from the Bible, taking into account the liturgical seasons. It is urged, moreover, that the individual conferences of bishops prepare lectionaries for Masses with children.

If because of the limited capabilities of the children it seems necessary to omit one or other verse of a biblical reading, this should be done cautiously and in such a way "that the meaning of the texts or the sense and, as it were, style of the scriptures are not mutilated."[41]

44. In the choice of readings the criterion to be followed is the quality rather than the quantity of the texts from the scriptures. In itself a shorter reading is not always more suited to children than a lengthy reading. Everything depends upon the spiritual advantage which the reading can offer to children.

45. In the biblical texts "God speaks to his people . . . and Christ himself is present

through his word in the assembly of the faithful."[42] Paraphrases of scripture should therefore be avoided. On the other hand, the use of translations which may already exist for the catechesis of children and which are accepted by the competent authority is recommended.

46. Verses of psalms, carefully selected in accord with the understanding of children, or singing in the form of psalmody or the alleluia with a simple verse should be sung between the readings. The children should always have a part in this singing, but sometimes a reflective silence may be substituted for the singing.

If only a single reading is chosen, there may be singing after the homily.

47. All the elements which will help to understand the readings should be given great consideration so that the children may make the biblical readings their own and may come more and more to appreciate the value of God's word.

Among these elements are the introductory comments which may precede the readings[43] and help the children to listen better and more fruitfully, either by explaining the context or by introducing the text itself. In interpreting and illustrating the readings from the scriptures in the Mass on a saint's day, an account of the life of the saint may be given not only in the homily but even before the readings in the form of a commentary.

Where the text of the readings suggest, it may be helpful to have the children read it with parts distributed among them, as is provided for the reading of the Lord's Passion during Holy Week.

48. The homily in which the word of God is unfolded should be given great prominence in all Masses with children. Sometimes the homily intended for children should become a dialogue with them, unless it is preferred that they should listen in silence.

49. If the profession of faith occurs at the end of the liturgy of the word, the Apostles' Creed may be used with children, especially because it is part of their catechetical formation.

c) Presidential Prayers

50. The priest is permitted to choose from the *Roman Missal* texts of presidential prayers more suited to children, keeping in mind the liturgical season, so that he may truly associate the children with himself.

51. Sometimes this principle of selection is insufficient if the children are to consider the prayers as the expression of their own lives and their own religious experience, since the prayers were composed for adult Christians.[44] In this case the text of prayers of the *Roman Missal* may be adapted to the needs of children, but this should be done in such a way that, preserving the purpose of the prayer and to some extent its substance as well, the priest avoids anything that is foreign to the literary genre of a presidential prayer, such as moral exhortations or a childish manner of speech.

52. The eucharistic prayer is of the greatest importance in the eucharist celebrated with children because it is the high point of the entire celebration.[45] Much depends upon the manner in which the priest proclaims this prayer[46] and in which the children take part by listening and making their acclamations.

The disposition of mind required for this central part of the celebration, the calm and reverence with which everything is done, should make the children as attentive as possible. They should be attentive to the real presence of Christ on the altar under the species of bread and wine, to his offering, to the thanksgiving through him and with him and in him, and to the offering of the Church which is made during the prayer and by which the faithful offer themselves and their lives with Christ to the eternal Father in the Holy Spirit.

For the present, the four eucharistic prayers approved by the supreme authority for Masses with adults are to be employed and kept in liturgical use until the Apostolic See makes other provision for Masses with children.

d) Rites before Communion
53. At the end of the eucharistic prayer, the Lord's Prayer, the breaking of bread, and the invitation to communion should always follow.[47] These elements have the principal significance in the structure of this part of the Mass.

e) Communion and the Following Rites
54. Everything should be done so that the children who are properly disposed and who have already been admitted to the eucharist may go to the holy table calmly and with recollection, so that they may take part fully in the eucharistic mystery. If possible there should be singing, accommodated to the understanding of children, during the communion procession.[48]

The invitation which precedes the final blessing[49] is important in Masses with children. Before they are dismissed they need some repetition and application of what they heard, but this should be done in a very few words. In particular, this is the appropriate time to express the connection between the liturgy and life.

At least sometimes, depending on the liturgical seasons and the different circumstances in the life of the children, the priest should use the richer forms of blessing, but he should always retain the trinitarian formula with the sign of the cross at the end.[50]

55. The contents of the directory are intended to help children quickly and joyfully to encounter Christ together in the eucharistic celebration and to stand in the presence of the Father with him.[51] If they are formed by conscious and active participation in the eucharistic sacrifice and meal, they should learn day by day, at home and away from home, to proclaim Christ to others among their family and among their peers, by living the "faith, which expresses itself through love" (Galatians 5:6).

This directory was prepared by the Congregation for Divine Worship. On October 22, 1973, the Supreme Pontiff, Paul VI, approved and confirmed it and ordered that it be made public.

From the office of the Congregation for Divine Worship, November 1, 1973, the solemnity of All Saints.

By special mandate of the Supreme Pontiff.

✠ Jean Card. Villot   ✠ A. Bugnini
 Secretary of State   Titular Archbishop of Diocletiana
                         Secretary of the Congregation for Divine Worship

NOTES

1. See Congregation for the Clergy, *Directorium Catechisticum Generale* (=DCG), no. 5: *AAS*, 64 (1972) 101-02.
2. See Vatican Council II, Constitution on the Liturgy, *Sacrosanctum Concilium* (=L), no. 33.

3. See DCG 78: *AAS*, 64 (1972) 146-47.

4. See L 38; also Congregation for Divine Worship, instruction *Actio pastoralis*, May 15, 1969: *AAS*, 61 (1969) 806-11.

5. First Synod of Bishops Liturgy, *Notitiae*, 3 (1967) 368.

6. See below, nos. 19, 32, 33.

7. See Order of Mass with children who are deaf-mutes for German-speaking countries, confirmed June 26, 1970, by this congregation (prot. no. 1546/70).

8. See L 14, 19.

9. See DCG 25: *AAS*, 64 (1972) 114.

10. See Vatican Council II, Declaration on Christian Education, *Gravissimum educationis*, no. 2.

11. See *Ibid.*, 3.

12. See DCG 78: *AAS*, 64 (1972) 147.

13. See L 33.

14. See Congregation of Rites, instruction *Eucharisticum mysterium* (=EM), May 25, 1967, no. 14: *AAS*, 59 (1967) 550.

15. See DCG 25: *AAS*, 64 (1972) 114.

16. See EM 14: *AAS*, 59 (1967) 550; also DCG 57: *AAS*, 64 (1972) 131.

17. See L 35, 4.

18. See above, no. 3.

19. See L 42, 106.

20. See first Synod of Bishops, Liturgy: *Notitiae*, 3 (1967) 368.

21. See General Instruction of the Roman Missal (=IG), no. 56.

22. See below, no. 37.

23. See IG 11.

24. See L 28.

25. See IG 253.

26. See IG 19.

27. See Congregation of Rites, instruction *Musicam sacram*, March 5, 1967, no. 55: *AAS*, 59 (1967) 316.

28. *Ibid.*, 62: *AAS*, 59 (1967) 318.

29. See above, no. 23.

30. See IG 21.

31. See IG 24.

32. See IG 23.

33. See instruction *Eucharisticum mysterium*, no. 38: *AAS*, 59 (1967) 562.

34. See IG 23.

35. See IG 8.

36. See L 48.

37. See above, no. 21.

38. IG 15.

39. IG 24.

40. IG 38.

41. See *Lectionary for Mass*, introduction, no. 7d.

42. IG 33.

43. See IG 11.

44. See Consilium for the Implementation of the Constitution on the Liturgy, Instruction on Translation of Liturgical Texts, January 25, 1969, no. 20: *Notitiae*, 5 (1969) 7.

45. See IG 54.

46. See above, nos. 23, 37.

47. See above, no. 23.

48. See instruction *Musicam sacram*, no. 32: *AAS*, 59 (1967) 309.

49. See IG 11.

50. See above, no. 39.

51. See Eucharistic Prayer II.

Appendix Two
Resource Bibliography
for Liturgies
with Young Christians
Mary Charles Bryce

Current interest in liturgies adapted to youthful congregations owes its beginnings to paragraph No. 38 in Vatican II's Constitution on the Sacred Liturgy (December 1963). That section allows "for legitimate variations and adaptations to different groups, regions and peoples. . . ."

At present there exists a wealth of material available for those who are involved in planning celebrations of the eucharist, reconciliation services and other sacramental events, where children outnumber or equal the participating adults. What follows here is not an exhaustive but a selected annotated bibliography which may be of assistance to pastors, parents and catechists. In some of the citations emphasis is placed on the parish assembly at worship. This is no mere accident for ideally speaking the Sunday celebration of the eucharist reaches and involves the entire congregation and each member responds in his and her own way at different levels.

OFFICIAL STATEMENTS AND COMMENTARIES
Approving the New Roman Missal and Instructions on Masses for Special Gatherings. Both of these were promulgated by the Vatican's Congregation for Divine Worship in 1969. They were published in English in that same year. Both are obtainable from the United States Catholic Conference, 1312 Massachusetts Ave., N.W., Washington, DC 20005.

Directory for Masses with Children. Sacred Congregation for Divine Worship (Promulgated November 1, 1973). Translated and obtainable from the United States Catholic Conference.

"Principles of Liturgical Adaptation," *Notitiae,* 10 (1974). Pope Paul VI decreed four general principles in response to requests for "new" eucharistic prayers in masses celebrated with children and masses of reconciliation (October 26, 1974). Those principles affect the areas of 1) signs; 2) translations; 3) music, singing; and 4) art.

Holmes, Urban T. *Young Children and the Eucharist.* New York: Seabury Press, 1972
($2.50 paper). Because Holmes writes so clearly and well about the importance of
symbol—"We cannot know God apart from the symbolic."—his work deserves
careful reading in the context of considering liturgies in which children make up
a large portion of the congregation.

Hovda, Robert. "The Eucharist is More than Words," *Living Worship,* 11 (April
1975). Hovda's article reminds us that good communication is not tied to wordiness.
Being mindful of that is essential to good celebrations with young Christians — and
older ones, too, for that matter.

Krosnicki, Thomas A., "The Directory for Masses with Children: A Commentary,"
The Living Light, 11 (Summer 1974). Krosnicki's scholarly and pastoral sensitivity
makes this article of special worth.

LeBlanc, Paul J., " 'Directory for Masses With Children' 'Purpose' of Elements Should
Correspond," *Living Worship,* 10 (May 1974).

Mead, Margaret, "Celebration: A Human Need," *The Catechist,* 1 (March 1968).
Insights from a noted anthropologist.

Eucharistic Prayers for Masses With Children. International Committee on English
in the Liturgy (1975). This 23-page "green book" with its three eucharistic prayers
originated with the ICEL group in Toronto, Canada. At this writing it has been
approved by the United States Catholic Conference and awaits final authorization
from Rome.

Study Text No. 4: New Rite of Penance. Washington: USCC, 1975. Promulgated by
the Bishops' Committee on the Liturgy. (41 pages, $1.50).

Crichton, J. D., *The Ministry of Reconciliation.* London: Geoffrey Chapman, 1974.
One of the assets to this volume is that it includes the church's document "New Rite
of Penance," as well as a commentary. Two other Crichton books deserve mention
here: They are his *Christian Celebration: The Mass* (1971) and *Christian Celebration: The Sacraments* (1973). Their special worth derives from the fact that Crichton has an excellent pastoral sense. The problem is that they are hard to locate in
this country.

Pottebaum, Gerard A., "The People's Rite to Change," *Liturgy,* 20 (February 1975).
An insightful article on the new penance rite and the Christian community's
involvement in ritual making.

_____. "The Art of Creating a Priestly People," *The Living Light,* 11 (Summer
1974).

TOWARD UNDERSTANDING CHILDREN

Keen, Sam. *Apology for Wonder.* New York: Harper & Row, 1968. Chapter 2,
"Childhood and Wonder," is particularly apropos here.

_____. *To a Dancing God.* New York; Harper & Row, 1970. If you haven't time to
read this entire book now, start with Chapter 3, "Reflections on a Peach Seed
Monkey . . ." for an appreciation of the enduring memory of childhood.

O'Gorman, Ned. *The Wilderness and the Laurel Tree.* New York: Harper Colophon
Books, 1972. This is a guide for children-watchers — or an encouragement to
become one.

Sharp, Evelyn. *Thinking is Child's Play.* New York: Avon Books, 1970. Another
volume to assist children-watchers understand those they are observing.

Steptoe, John. *Stevie.* New York: Harper & Row, 1969. This is a story for children.
Grown-ups might appreciate it even more. It's helpful in looking at the meaning
of reconciliation.

IDEA READINGS

Berube, Francoise Darcy and Berube, John Paul. *Sacrament of Peace*. New York: Paulist Press, 1974. This 120-page book is part of a four-volume program on penance. The following texts complete the series: *A Guide for Parents; An Illustrated Booklet for Children 7 and 8 years old; An Illustrated Booklet for Children 9 to 12 years old.*

Bloy, Myron, Jr. (ed.). *Multi-Media Worship*. New York: Seabury Press, 1969. This inexpensive work offers a model and numerous ideas.

Bonin, Edmond (trans.). *The Good News for Children*. Dayton: Pflaum/Standard, 1968. Simple excerpts for children 6-8 years of age.

Brown, John. *New Ways in Worship for Youth*. Valley Forge, PA: Judson Press, 1970. This is a resource book for planning worship with teenagers.

Carroll, James. *Wonder and Worship*. New York: Newman Press, 1970. An attempt to stir the sense of wonder and celebration by telling the story in different ways. The author's opening words challenge and engage one: "Our world will not be wonderful until we ourselves are full of wonder."

Coleman, William V. and McLemore, Patricia R. *God Believes in Me*. Notre Dame: Ave Maria Press, 1974. Selected lesson headings speak for themselves: "God Loves Me"; "God Believes in Me"; "God Believes I Can Be Like Jesus"; "God Speaks to Me Through the Sacrament of Penance."

Faucher, W. Thomas and Nieland, Ione C. *Touching God*. Notre Dame: Ave Maria Press, 1975. The two authors of this work offer a valuable resource and idea book. Besides 17 model liturgies for young congregations, planning suggestions, and helpful hints to the celebrants, they have included the complete text of the *Directory for Masses With Children* and an explanation and commentary on that document.

Huck, Gabe. *Celebrate Summer: A Guidebook for Families*. New York: Paulist/ Newman, 1973.

Jeep, Elizabeth and Huck, Gabe. *Celebrate Summer: A Guidebook for Congregations*. New York: Paulist Press, 1973. The hot months of summer put no limitations on these two volumes. Within their covers they contain ideas that can be used throughout the year and challenge their users to be creative on their own.

Hynes, Arlene. *The Passover Meal*. New York: Paulist Press, 1972. This pamphlet is adapted for use by Christian families.

LeBlanc, Etienne and Talbot, Mary Rose. *How Green is Green?* Notre Dame: Ave Maria Press, n.d.

Rabelais, Maria. *Children Celebrate*. New York: Paulist Press, 1975.

_____. *Come, Be Reconciled*. New York: Paulist Press, 1975. Both of these volumes have proven their worth in the Diocese of Baton Rouge, LA. They offer guidelines, suggestions, models and ideas for eucharist and penance celebrations for children of all ages.

Rochelle, Joy. *Create and Celebrate*. Philadelphia: Fortress Press, 1971. A helpful resource book for planning liturgies.

Sloyan, Virginia and Huck, Gabe. *Children's Liturgies*. Washington, D.C.: Liturgical Conference, 1970. One of the earliest and most comprehensive works on the concept of liturgies for young children this book remains a classic. Its sequel (which follows here) only extends that excellence.

_____. *Signs, Songs, Stories*. Washington, D.C.: Liturgical Press, 1974.

Stantan, Frances. *Meet God and Live*. Derby, NY: St. Paul Publishers, 1969. Idea source for high school liturgies.

SELECTED ARTICLES
Collins, Patrick W., Hoffman, Eleanor and Coopman, Ruth, "Can the Community Liturgy Really Involve Children?" *Liturgy,* 19 (April 1974) 27-28.
Gusmer, Charles W. and students, "SG 504: (or) How to Celebrate the Symbols of Christian Initiation," *Liturgy,* 20 (January 1974), 8-20.
National Center for Religious Education, CCD. "Planning the Sacrament of Penance With Younger Children," *The Living Light,* 10 (Winter 1973), 597-603.

NEWSLETTERS
Children's Liturgy. A quarterly newsletter ($2 per year, prepaid) published by Committee on Children's Liturgy, P.O. Box 2108, Baton Rouge, LA 70821.
Worship Resources Newsletter. This informative monthly is in its third year of publication. The December 1974 issue had a special reference to celebrating the liturgy with youth. Address: 1596 West Woodman Road, Colorado Springs, CO 80919 ($3 per year).

LECTIONARIES
Behnke, John. *A Children's Lectionary: Cycle A.* New York: Paulist Press, 1974. Written for the purpose of helping teachers prepare children for the Sunday liturgies. Useful within that framework; it is not recommended for use in the celebration.
Tos, Aldo J. *Lectionary for Children's Mass.* New York: Pueblo Press, 1974. Scripture texts are left intact in this volume but only two (including the gospel pericope) are included for each Sunday's celebration. Because of type style and spacing it is easy reading. (1860 Broadway, New York, NY 10023).

MUSIC RESOURCES
Alexander, Peloquin. *Mass of the Bells.* Gregorian Institute of America. The *Gloria,* with its oft-repeated initial phrase, lends itself beautifully to antiphonal singing with a choir and full congregation. Children quickly learn the refrain, "Glory to God in the highest. . . ."
Blunt, Neil; Miffleton, Jack; Blandford, Sr. Elizabeth; Bucher, Sr. Janet Marie. *Come Out Kit.* Cincinnati: World Library Publications, Inc., 1971. Planned for children 2-8 years of age this kit offers cut-out sheets, posters, record and songbook. The total kit sells for $10.95, but sections can be purchased separately. World Library Publications, 2145 Central Pkwy., Cincinnati, OH 45214.
Catholic Book of Worship. Canadian Catholic Conference. Produced and distributed by Gordon V. Thompson, Ltd., 29 Birch Avenue, Toronto 7, Ont., Canada. With its numerous and wide variety this hymnal offers a wealth of singable and appropriate hymns for both the youthful and mature in a congregation.
Isele, Wm. *Song in Sacrament.* Cincinnati: North American Liturgy Resources, 1971 ($1.25). 300 East McMillan Street, Cincinnati, OH 45219.
Kiefer, Ralph (Ed.). *Catholic Liturgy Book.* Baltimore: Helicon, 1975. A compact volume with about one-half of its contents devoted to hymns, acclamations, etc., it sells itself as a *good* parish hymnal. Because of the natural rhythmic sense that most children possess, the CLB songs readily appeal to the younger generation
Life, Love, Joy Series. Recorded music numbers from volumes for grades 1-3, 5. Florham Park, NJ: Silver Burdett Co., P.O. Box 39, 07932.
Medical Mission Sisters. *Joy Is Like the Rain. I Know the Secret. Seasons.* New York: Vanguard Music Corp. These records, which one may also purchase the melody-

text edition, piano-unison-vocal edition and the guitar edition, are particularly good for selected gospel narrations in melodic form. They have an enduring quality which attracts children.

New Life and *On Our Way*. These series have music selections for each of the grades in the elementary level. Wm. J. Sadlier, Inc., 11 Park Place, New York, NY 10007.

FILMS

The Gulf. Mass Media Ministries, 2116 Charles St., Baltimore, MD 21218. The distance and depth between two cliffs creates the obstacle to interpersonal communications for two bouncing busybodies who look exactly alike except for their color and who are most eager to get close enough to converse. Concerns the Christian meaning of neighborliness and understanding. (Color, 3 min., 1973, rental: $7.50, sale: $75.)

O Happy Day! The "liberator" in this delightful celebration film is a street sweeper, a garbage collector whose presence touches and somehow changes everyone he meets. Could be used for junior high to adults in both worship and discussion settings. (Color, 10 min., rental: $15; sale: $150.)

What Hands Can Do. Mass Media Ministries, 1968. Children's hands perform all the roles in this beautifully photographed three-act play that tells of the endless variety of uses for hands. (Color, 10 min., rental: $12.)

DIOCESAN GUIDELINES, DIRECTIVES, ETC.

Diocese of Baltimore, MD. *Repent and Believe*. (1971) Penance service for the church year according to age groups. 75¢. 320 Cathedral Street, Baltimore, MD 21201.

Diocese of Baton Rouge. Committee on Children's Liturgy. Among other activities this committee produces a quarterly newsletter (see above).

Archdiocese of Chicago. *Seven Penitential Services* (1971). Liturgy training program, 5947 N. Manton Ave., Chicago, IL 60646. 75¢.

Diocese of Grand Rapids. *Penance Celebrations for Children*. Edited by Sr. Teresa Mahony (1972). Diocesan School Office, 350 Sheldon Ave., SE, Grand Rapids, MI 49502.

Diocese of Lansing. *Living the Liturgy Daybook, Vol. I* (1971). This volume includes suggestions for prayers, customs, etc. for home, parish and school. It begins with Advent, concludes with Easter. Liturgical Commission, 300 West Ottawa, Lansing, MI 48933. $6

Diocese of Youngstown. *A Commentary on the Directory for Masses With Children* (1974).

Bibliography from: *Living Light* 12 (1975): 461-67
compiled by Mary Charles Bryce, O.S.B.
reprinted with permission

Supplementary Bibliography
1975–80

This collection is an update and supplement to the "Resource Bibliography for Liturgies with Young Christians," by Mary Charles Bryce.

BOOKS

Bucher, Janet Marie. *Run With Him.* Cincinnati: North American Liturgy Resources, 1974.

Durka, Gloria, and Smith, Joanmarie. *Aesthetic Dimensions of Religious Education.* New York: Paulist Press, 1979. A thorough study of the role of creativity in catechesis.

Freburger, William J., and Haas, James E. *Eucharistic Prayers for Children.* Notre Dame: Ave Marie Press, 1976. A collection of model liturgies.

Jasper, Ronald C. D., ed. *Worship and the Child.* London: SPCK, 1975. Scholarly essays by the English Joint Liturgical Group.

Neville, Gwen Kennedy, and Westhoff, John H. *Learning Through Liturgy.* New York: The Seabury Press, 1978. Liturgy as part of the educational process.

Pratt, Oliver. *Let Liturgy Live.* London: Sheed and Ward, 1973.

Sloyan, Virginia. *Signs, Songs and Stories: Another Look at Children's Liturgies.* Washington D.C.: The Liturgical Conference, 1974.

Westerhoff, John H., and Williamson, Willimon H. *Liturgy and Learning Through the Life Cycle.* New York: Seabury Press, 1980.

FOR CHILDREN OF THE EASTERN CHURCHES

Chakos, John. *The Joyful Feast.* Brookline: Greek Orthodox Archidiocese of North and South America, 1978.

Divine Liturgy Book. Brookline: Greek Orthodox Archdiocese of North and South America, 1976. The Divine Liturgy is presented in Greek, English, and through drawings.

Koulomzin, Sophie. *Our Church and Our Children.* Crestwood, N.Y.: SVS Press, 1975.

Schmemann, Alexander. *Liturgy and Life: Christian Development through Liturgical Experience.* Syosset, N.Y.: Orthodox Church in America, 1974.

_____. *Of Water and the Spirit: A Liturgical Study of Baptism.* Crestwood: SVS Press, 1974.

PERIODICAL LITERATURE
Bryce, Mary Charles,O.S.B."Liturgy and Young Christians." *Catechist* 9 (1975) pp. 18–22.
_____. "The Interrelationship of Liturgy and Catechesis." *American Benedictine Review* 25 (1977): pp. 1–29.
Craghan, John F. "The Preacher and Children." *The Bible Today*, Sept. 1979.
Durkin, Mary G., "Prayer and Spirituality: Prayer Life and Children," *Today's Catholic Teacher*, April 1979, pp. 38–9.
Ennis, Margot, and Laurent, Margaret. "Children's Liturgy for your Parish." *Today's Parish*, April (1979), pp. 36–8.
Hayeland, James A. "A Children's Liturgy for Christmas." *Today's Parish*, Nov.–Dec. 11 (1979), pp. 42–3.
Hiesburger, Jean Marie. "What We forget About Young People." *Liturgy* 24 (1979): pp. 35–7.
Keefe, Jeffrey. "The Psychology of Religious Experience." *Catechist* Feb. 12 (1979): pp. 23ff.
McKenna, Edward J. "Peloquin for Children: Premier of 'Unless You Become.' " *Liturgy* Nov.–Dec., 1979, pp. 32–3.
Miles, Michael. "Sunday's Children: Homilies Involving Children's Insights." *Modern Liturgy* May 1978, pp. 32–3.
Wiebler, William. "Homilies for Children." *Today's Parish* Jan. 11 (1977): pp. 11–12.

SPECIAL ISSUES
(The following are periodicals which have devoted substantial portions of a particular issue to Children's Liturgy.)
Liturgy vol. 24. July–August 1979. Contains several articles relevant to Children's Liturgy.
Living Light vol. 12. 1975. The entire Fall issue is devoted to Worship for Young People. It is in this issue that the aforementioned Bryce Bibliography appears.
Modern Liturgy vol. 5. May 1978. "Family Liturgy Symposium."
Modern Liturgy vol. 5 Sept.–Oct. 1977. "Liturgy and Youth Symposium."